SAMSUNG

MW01097407

User Guide

[UG template version 15b]

[Boost-Samsung-J320P-UM-EN-122315-FINAL]

Introduction

The following topics describe the basics of using this guide and your new phone.

About the User Guide

Thank you for purchasing your new Samsung Galaxy® J3 (2016). The following topics explain how best to use this guide to get the most out of your phone.

Before Using Your Phone

Read the Get Started guide and Important Information booklet that were packaged with your phone thoroughly for proper usage.

Accessible services may be limited by subscription contract conditions.

Descriptions in the User Guide

Note that most descriptions in this guide are based on your phone's setup at the time of purchase. Unless otherwise noted, instructions begin from the phone's home screen, which is displayed by pressing the **Home** key. Some operation descriptions may be simplified.

Screenshots and Key Labels

Screenshots in the user guide may appear differently on your phone. Key labels in the user guide are simplified for description purposes and may differ from your phone's display.

Other Notations

In the user guide, the phone may be referred to either as "phone," "device," or "handset."

Get Support from Boost Zone

Access support for your phone and service through the preloaded Boost Zone app.

1. From home, tap **Apps** ⊞ > **Boost Zone** 🔲.

2. From the Boost Zone main page, tap **My Account**.

3. Tap a topic to view its contents.

Get Started

The following topics give you all the information you need to set up your phone and wireless service the first time.

Parts and Functions

These topics illustrate your phone's primary parts and key functions.

Phone Layout

The following illustration outlines your phone's primary external features and buttons.

Front View

Part	Description
Earpiece	Listen to calls and automated prompts when using the phone.
Proximity sensors	Detect when objects are close to the screen. For example, when you hold the phone to your ear while on a phone call, the sensors temporarily lock the screen to prevent accidental screen touches.
Front camera	Takes pictures and records videos while facing the screen, and allows you to video conference.

Part	Description
Power/Lock key	Turn the phone or screen on or off, enable Airplane mode, or Restart the phone.
Back key ⬅	Return you to the previous screen, or close a dialog box, options menu, the notification panel, or the keyboard.
Home key	Returns you to the home screen.
Recent Apps key ⬜	Access recently used apps.
Touchscreen	Display information needed to operate your phone, such as the call status, the Contacts list, and the date and time. Also provides one-tap access to all of your features and applications.
Volume key	Adjust the ringtone or media volume or adjust the voice volume during a call.

Rear View

Microphone
Headset jack
Flash
Speaker
Rear camera
Microphone
USB charger/accessory port

Part	Description
Microphone	Transmit your voice for phone calls or record your voice or ambient sounds for voice recordings and videos. There are two microphones, one on the top and one on the bottom.

Part	Description
Headset jack	Plug in a headset for convenient, hands-free conversations.
Speaker	Play ringtones and sounds. The speaker also lets you hear the caller's voice in speakerphone mode.
Rear camera	Take pictures and videos.
USB charger/accessory port	Connect the phone to the charger using a USB cable.
Flash	Help illuminate subjects in low-light environments when the camera is focusing and capturing a picture or video.

Caution! Inserting an accessory into the incorrect jack may damage the phone.

Set Up Your Phone

You must first install and charge the battery to begin setting up your phone.

Note: It is recommended you fully charge the battery before using your device for the first time.

1. Install the battery.

    - Using the slot provided, gently lift the cover off the phone.

    - Insert the battery, aligning the gold contacts on the battery with the gold contacts on the phone, and gently press the battery into place.

    - Insert an optional SD card, see microSD card for more information.

    - Replace the back cover, making sure all the tabs are secure and that there are no gaps around the cover.

Warning: Do not bend or twist the back cover excessively. Doing so may damage the cover.

2. Plug the USB cable into the USB charger/accessory port on the bottom of the phone.

3. Plug the other end of the USB cable into the charging head, and then plug the charging head into an electrical outlet to charge your battery. Fully charging a battery may take several hours.

Note: Your phone's battery should have enough charge to turn the phone on and find a signal, run the setup application, set up voicemail, and make a call. You should fully charge the battery as soon as possible.

Caution: Use only Samsung-approved charging devices and batteries. Samsung accessories are designed to maximize battery life. Using other accessories may invalidate your warranty and may cause damage.

Caution: Failure to unplug the wall charger before you remove the battery may cause damage to the device.

4. Press and hold the **Power/Lock** key to turn the phone on.

    ▪ If your phone is activated, it will turn on, search for network service, and begin the setup application.

5. If your phone is not yet activated, see Activation and Service for more information.

Turn Your Phone On and Off

The instructions below explain how to turn your phone on and off.

Turn Your Phone On

■ Press and hold the **Power/Lock** key.

Power/Lock key

❖ Your phone will power on. Depending on the settings, you may see the lock screen.

▪ See Lock and Unlock Your Screen and Screen Lock for information about using the screen lock.

▪ The first time you turn the phone on, you will see the startup screens. See Complete the Setup Screens for details.

▪ If your phone is not yet activated, see Activation and Service for more information.

Turn Your Phone Off

1. Press and hold the **Power/Lock** key to open the phone options menu.

Power/Lock key

2. Tap **Power off** > **Power off** to turn the phone off.

❖ Your phone will power off.

Your screen remains blank while your phone is off (unless the battery is charging).

Tip: If your device is not responding, press and hold both the **Power/Lock** key and **Volume down** key simultaneously for more than seven seconds to restart the device.

Use the Touchscreen

Your phone's touchscreen lets you control actions through a variety of touch gestures.

Tap or Touch

When you want to type using the keyboard, select items such as application and settings icons, or press buttons, simply tap or touch them with your finger.

Touch and Hold

To open the available options for an item (for example, a contact or link in a Web page), touch and hold the item.

Swipe or Slide

To swipe or slide means to quickly drag your finger vertically or horizontally across the screen.

Drag

To drag, press and hold your finger with some pressure before you start to move your finger. While dragging, do not release your finger until you have reached the target position.

Flick

Flicking the screen is similar to swiping, except that you need to move your finger in light, quick strokes. This finger gesture is always in a vertical direction, such as when flicking the contacts or message list.

Rotate

For most screens, you can automatically change the screen orientation from portrait to landscape by turning the phone sideways. When entering text, you can turn the phone sideways to bring up a bigger keyboard. See Enter Text for more details.

Note: Auto rotate must be enabled for the screen orientation to automatically change. To enable screen rotation, slide your finger down from the status bar to display the notification panel, and then tap **Auto rotate** to enable the option.

Pinch and Spread

Pinch the screen by moving two fingers inward to zoom out, or spread by moving two fingers outward to zoom in.

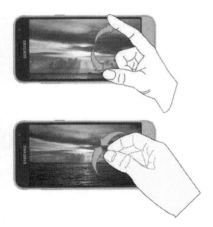

Activation and Service

Before using your phone, you must set up your service with Boost Mobile. You will need your phone's serial number (MEID), printed on a sticker inside the battery compartment.

For more information about your Boost Mobile account, see Boost Account Information and Help.

Create Your Account and Pick Your Plan

Set up your Boost Mobile account.

1. From your computer, visit boostmobile.com/activate.

2. Choose an activation option and click **Next**.

3. When prompted, enter the serial number (MEID) printed on the sticker located on the back of your phone in the battery compartment. This number can also be found on the bottom panel of the phone's package.

4. Follow the prompts to choose your plan and select a payment method.

5. Follow the activation instructions below and you will be able to start using your phone.

Note: You can also activate by phone by calling **1-888-BOOST-4U** (1-888-266-7848) from any other phone.

Activate Your Phone

After setting up your account on boostmobile.com, simply turn your device on. Your device is designed to activate automatically. If you are swapping from another Boost Mobile device to a new one, be sure to turn off the old device before swapping the serial number (MEID). Once the MEID swap is complete, turn on the new device and the programming information will be pushed to your device automatically.

You can also start the activation process manually.

- From home, tap **Apps** ⊞ > **Settings** ⚙ > **Activate this device** ⬇.

Complete the Setup Screens

The setup screens help you set up certain features and preferences on your phone. Once your phone has been turned on, you will see a Welcome message. You can then complete the setup process.

Note: You may be able to complete the setup screens before your phone has been activated on your Boost account.

1. At the Welcome screen, choose options, and then tap ⬤ to begin setup:

   - **Language**: Choose the default language for your phone's operation.

   - **Accessibility**: Configure settings to improve the accessibility of your phone's features if you are visually impaired or hard of hearing.

- **Emergency call**: Make an emergency call.

2. Follow the prompts to complete setup for each topic. Tap **Next**, or the right arrow, to move through the steps. You can skip options to continue to the next one. During setup, you may see the following options:

Note: Screens may vary based on the activation status of your phone.

- **Wi-Fi**: By default, your phone prompts you to use Wi-Fi when accessing data services. Tap a Wi-Fi access point to connect to it, or you can continue setup using your phone's connection to the wireless network.

- **Terms and conditions**: Read the End User License Agreement (EULA) and then tap **Agree** to confirm that you understand and agree to the terms and conditions. If you do not agree to the EULA, you cannot continue with setup.

    - If you consent to provide diagnostic and usage data to Samsung, tap the check box.

- **Hands Free Activation**: Automatically connect to the network and set up voice and data services.

    - After Hands Free Activation completes, tap **OK** to continue.

    - You may see a message indicating your phone needs to restart. Tap **OK** again and wait for your phone to restart.

- **Add your account (Google)**: Your phone uses your Google Account to provide access to many features and apps. Complete the steps to sign in to your current Google Account, or sign up for a new Google Account right from your phone. You can also skip signing in to your Google Account, or sign in later.

    - To sign in to an existing Google Account, you will need your account name (Gmail address) and password.

    - For both new and existing accounts, you will need to review and accept the Terms of Service and Privacy Policy by tapping **Accept** when prompted.

- **Date & time**: Configure your time zone, date, and time, if necessary.

- **Name**: Enter your First and Last name, to personalize Google features and apps.

- **Protect your phone**: Set up a screen lock to prevent others from using the phone without your permission.

- **Google services**: Select Google service preferences, including Backup & Restore, Location and Communication options.

- **Samsung account**: Some apps and features use your Samsung account. You can sign in to your Samsung account, or follow the prompts to create a new account.

    - To sign in to or set up a Samsung account, you will have to review and agree to the Terms and Conditions by tapping **Agree** when prompted.

- **Easy mode**: Easy mode offers a simpler home screen layout, with larger text and icons. Tap **ON/OFF** to turn on Easy mode. You can also choose Easy mode from Settings at any time.

3. Tap **Finish** to complete setup.

- Your phone is now set up for use. If you skipped any part of the setup, you can access additional options through the Apps list or through Settings.

Note: You do not need to sign up for a Google Account to use your phone. However, to download apps from the Google Play store app, you must link your phone to a Google Account.

Basic Operations

The following topics outline basic features and operations of your phone.

Basics

The following topics offer an overview of your phone's basic operations.

Home Screen and Applications (Apps) List

Most of your phone's operations originate from the home screen or the apps list.

1. From any screen, press the **Home** key to display the home screen.

2. Tap **Apps** ⊞ to display the apps list.

Home screen   Apps list

For information about using the home screen, see Home Screen Basics.

Select Options and Navigate Screens

Tap icons, keys, and other items to open or activate the assigned function.

- Tap the **Back** key ⮌ to return to the previous screen.

Recent Applications

You can display a list of recently used applications using the Recent Apps key.

- Tap the **Recent Apps** key □ to view a list of recently used applications.

Phone Settings Menu

You can customize your phone's settings and options through the Settings menu.

- From home, tap **Apps** ⊞ > **Settings** ⚙.

– or –

Drag the notification panel down and tap **Settings** ⚙.

- ❖ The Settings menu displays.

For more information, see Settings.

Portrait and Landscape Screen Orientation

The default orientation for your phone's screen is portrait (vertical), but many apps will change to landscape orientation (widescreen) when you rotate the phone sideways.

Turn Screen Rotation On or Off

1. Open the notification panel by dragging down from the top of the screen.

2. Tap **Screen rotation** 🔄 to turn the option on or off.

   - You may need to scroll left or right to see the Auto rotate option.

   - If the Screen rotation option is not available, tap **Edit** 🖊 to display the full options list.

   - Not all screens will adjust for landscape orientation.

Capture Screenshots

You can use your phone's Power/Lock key and Home key to capture screenshots.

- Press and hold the **Power/Lock** key and **Home** key at the same time to capture a screenshot of the current screen.

  ❖ The current screenshot will be captured and stored in the Screenshots album in the phone's Gallery. From home, tap **Apps** ⊞ > **Gallery** 🖼.

Applications

The following topics describe how to access the applications (apps) list and launch apps on your phone.

Launch Applications

All installed apps can be accessed and launched from the apps list.

1. From home, tap **Apps** .

❖ The apps list opens.

2. Tap an app icon to launch the corresponding application.

❖ The application opens.

Tip: Swipe left to view additional apps list screens. Some apps may reside within folders in the apps list; to open these, tap the folder and then tap the app icon.

Apps List

The apps list expands to include any apps you download and install on your phone. The following table outlines the primary apps that have been preinstalled on your phone.

App	Function/Service
1Weather	Receive real-time local weather information at any location in the world. Access 7-day and hourly weather forecasts for your area.
airG	Meet new friends instantly with just one click. Real-time feeds allow you to browse through the latest community activity or just see what your friends are up to.
Boost 411	Boost 411 gives you access to a variety of services and information, including residential, business, and government listings; movie listings or show times; driving directions, restaurant reservations, and major local event information. You can get up to three pieces of information per call, and the operator can automatically connect your call at no additional charge.

App	Function/Service
Boost Music	Discover millions of DRM-free music tracks, ringtones, and ringback tones from Boost's official music store and player.
Boost Wallet	Boost Wallet is a quick and easy way to make payments with cash directly from your Boost Mobile phone. Send money, pay bills and top-up your mobile phone account balance.
boostTV	Watch live and on demand entertainment from popular broadcast and cable networks, news channels and primetime TV shows.
Boost Zone	Stay connected to all the latest news and information from Boost. Included here are news, feedback, featured applications and tips/tricks for your device.
Calculator	Perform basic and advanced mathematical calculations.
Calendar	Use Calendar to create and manage events, meetings, and appointments, organize your time, and be reminded of important events.
CallWatch	Receive alerts in real-time of suspicious and unwanted incoming calls and text messages.
Camera	Take pictures and record videos using the front and rear cameras.
Chrome	Browse the Internet using Google's Chrome Web browser.
Clock	Set alarms, view time in time zones around the world, use a stopwatch, set a timer, and use your phone as a desk clock.
Contacts	Store and manage contacts from a variety of sources, including contacts you enter and save directly in your phone as well as contacts synchronized with your Google Account, compatible email programs (including Exchange Server), and your Facebook friends.
Drive	Store, sync, and access your data across multiple devices with Google Drive's cloud storage. Located in the Google folder in the apps list.
Email	Send and receive email from a variety of email service providers.
Facebook	Keep up with friends and family with the Facebook app. Share updates, photos, and videos, as well as text, chat, and play games.
Gadget Guardian	Keep your device and personal data safe and secure.

Basic Operations

App	Function/Service
Galaxy Apps	Discover apps designed exclusively for your Galaxy device.
Gallery	View and edit pictures and watch videos that you have taken with your phone's camera or downloaded.
Gmail	Send and receive messages using Google's Gmail service. Located in the Google folder in the apps list.
Google	Search the Internet using the Google app. Located in the Google folder in the apps list.
Google Settings	Use Google Settings to manage your Google apps and account settings. Located in the Google folder in the apps list.
Hangouts	Instant message with your friends and family using Google Hangouts. Located in the Google folder in the apps list.
Instagram	Capture and share photos and videos with your friends. Customize what you capture, and then share it on your feed or post it directly to your friends.
Internet	Browse the Internet using a full-featured browser.
Maps	Use Google Maps to determine your current location with or without GPS, get driving and transit directions, and find phone numbers and addresses for local businesses.
Memo	Organize your life by creating, editing, and managing memos. Located in the Tools folder in the apps list.
Messages	Send and receive text and multimedia messages.
Messaging Plus	Messaging Plus provides high quality video calling, group chat, and media sharing along with easy registration, a full emoji keyboard, and other convenient features.
Messenger	Instantly reach your friends and family with Facebook Messenger.
Microsoft Excel	Create and share spreadsheets quickly and easily with Microsoft Excel. Located in the Microsoft Apps folder in the apps list.
Microsoft OneDrive	OneDrive gives you free online storage for all your personal files so you can get to them from your Android device, computer, and any other devices you use. Located in the Microsoft Apps folder in the apps list.

App	Function/Service
Microsoft OneNote	Stay organized using text, pictures, or audio notes. Create Quick Notes or review and edit shared OneNote notebooks using OneDrive. Located in the Microsoft Apps folder in the apps list.
Microsoft PowerPoint	Create and share presentations quickly and easily with Microsoft PowerPoint. Located in the Microsoft Apps folder in the apps list.
Microsoft Word	Create and share word processing documents quickly and easily with Microsoft Word. Located in the Microsoft Apps folder in the apps list.
My Files	Manage your sounds, images, videos, Bluetooth files, Android files, and other data in one convenient location. Located in the Tools folder in the apps list.
NextRadio	Listen to your favorite local radio stations with NextRadio – FM radio on your smartphone. Tune in to any FM frequency in your area and listen to the radio without the buffering and cost of streaming music.
Pages Manager	Manage up to 50 social media pages from your smartphone or tablet with the Pages Manager app. You can check page activity, share with your audience and see insights.
Phone	Make and receive phone calls.
Photos	View photos and videos on your phone, and sync them with your Google+ account. Located in the Google folder in the apps list.
Play Movies & TV	Use Google Play Movies & TV to watch movies and TV shows purchased on Google Play. You can stream instantly on your Android phone or download so you can watch from anywhere, even when you are not connected. Located in the Google folder in the apps list.
Play Music	Use the Google Play Music app to browse, shop, and play back songs purchased from Google Play as well as songs you have loaded from your own music library.
Play Store	Use the Google Play store app to find new Android apps, games, movies, music, and books for your phone. Choose from a wide variety of free and paid apps ranging from productivity apps to games.
Samsung Milk Music	Samsung Milk Music is a streaming radio service that offers a simple way to find the music that is right for you. With a library of over 13 million songs and 200+ stations, the interactive dial makes it easy to skim through stations, to find the perfect soundtrack for the moment.

App	Function/Service
Settings	Configure settings and options on your phone.
Uber	Search and find transportation service using the Uber app. Request a ride and get picked up within minutes.
Video	View videos on your phone.
Voice Recorder	Record voice memos and share them with others. Located in the Tools folder in the apps list.
Voice Search	Search the Internet and your phone using voice commands. Located in the Google folder in the apps list.
Voicemail	Use Visual Voicemail for a quick and easy way to access your voicemail. Now you can find exactly the message you are looking for without having to listen to every voicemail message first.
YouTube	Access the YouTube video sharing website on which users can upload and share videos. The site is used to display a wide variety of user-generated video content, including movie clips, TV clips, and music videos, as well as video content such as video blogging, informational shorts, and other original videos.

Note: Available apps are subject to change.

Phone Number

Follow the instructions below to display your phone's wireless phone number.

1. From home, tap **Apps** ⊞ > **Settings** ⚙ > **About device** ⓘ.

2. Tap **Status** > **Sim card status**.

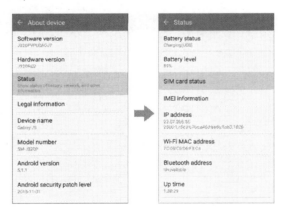

❖ You will see the number listed under **My phone number**.

Airplane Mode

Airplane mode turns off all functions that emit or receive signals, while leaving your phone on so you can use apps that do not require a signal or data.

To turn on Airplane mode:

1. Press and hold the **Power/Lock** key to display the device options menu.

2. Tap **Airplane mode** > **Turn on** to turn Airplane mode on.

   ❖ Your phone is now in Airplane mode. An Airplane mode icon ✈ displays on the status bar.

Tip: You can also turn on Airplane mode through the notification panel. Drag the status bar down to reveal the notification panel, slide the Quick settings buttons to the left, and then tap **Airplane mode** 🛇 > **Turn on** to turn Airplane mode on.

To turn off Airplane mode:

1. Press and hold the **Power/Lock** key to display the device options menu.

2. Tap **Airplane mode**.

   ❖ Your phone's wireless connection features are now restored.

Tip: You can also turn off Airplane mode through the notification panel. Slide the status bar down to reveal the notification panel, slide the Quick settings buttons to the left, and then tap **Airplane mode** 🛇 to turn Airplane mode off.

Enter Text

You can type on your phone using the touchscreen Samsung keyboard or Google voice typing.

Samsung Keyboard

Use the touchscreen Samsung keyboard for entering text. The keyboard appears automatically when you tap a text entry field, and can be used in either portrait or landscape mode. You can also use the Google voice typing option to enter text using your voice (see Google Voice Typing for details).

The Samsung keyboard offers a traditional QWERTY keyboard setup for entering text by tapping keys (like on a computer), along with enhancements and options that allow you to enter text faster and more accurately, such as continuous key input, personalized usage dictionaries, and more.

| Portrait | Landscape |

Note: Depending on which app you are using (Messages, Email, and more), the keyboard appearance may differ.

Assigning the Samsung Keyboard for Text Entry

If you have multiple text input methods installed on your device, you can select the Samsung keyboard to be your default text input method from Settings, or you can choose it at any time while entering text.

Note: The Samsung keyboard is the default text input method on your phone. Additional keyboards and input methods are available for download at the Google Play store. See Google Play Store.

From Settings:

- From home, tap **Apps** ⊞ > **Settings** ⚙ > **Language and input** ⓐ > **Default keyboard**, and then choose **Samsung keyboard**.

While entering text:

1. While entering text, drag down from the top of the screen to open the notification panel.

2. Tap **Select keyboard**, and then choose Samsung keyboard.

Use Samsung Keyboard to Enter Text

- Tap keys to enter text. While entering text, use the following options:

  - If you make a mistake, tap ⌫ to delete incorrect characters. Touch and hold ⌫ to delete a whole word or field.

- Tap ⬆ to change the case of the text (the arrow will turn blue). Tap ⬆ twice to switch to all capitals (the key will turn blue).

- Tap Sym to switch to a symbols keyboard. There are two symbol keyboards; to switch between them, tap 1/2 or 2/2.

- Tap 🎤 to switch to Google voice typing to enter text by speaking. See Google Voice Typing.

- Touch and hold 🎤 to open an options menu. Select from the following options:

  - 🎤 **Google voice typing** to switch to Google voice typing.

  - 😊 **Emoticon** to display a list of emoticons.

  - ⚙ **Settings** to view the Samsung keyboard settings menu.

- If you have more than one language selected in Samsung keyboard settings, you can swipe your finger over English(US) to switch between languages.

Configure Samsung Keyboard

- From home, tap **Apps** ⊞ > **Settings** ⚙ > **Language and input** Ⓐ > **Samsung keyboard**.

Google Voice Typing

Google voice typing uses Google voice recognition to convert speech to text.

Use Google Voice Typing to Enter Text

1. While entering text, drag down from the top of the screen to open the notification panel, and then tap **Select keyboard** > **Google voice typing**.

   – or –

   Tap 🎤 on the Samsung keyboard.

   – or –

   Touch and hold 🎤 on the Samsung keyboard, and then tap 🎤.

2. Speak into the microphone and watch your text being entered.

3. If the text is incorrect, tap **Delete** 🔲.

4. Once you have completed entering your text, tap ✕. The keyboard will reappear.

Note: You can assign a new language to Google voice typing. Tap ⚙ > **Languages** and tap a language to select it.

Configure Google Voice Typing

- From home, tap **Apps** ▦ > **Settings** ⚙ > **Language and input** Ⓐ > **Google voice typing**.

Tips for Editing Text

Your phone gives you many options to make entering text easier, including copying, cutting, and pasting text, using voice-to-text input, customizing the user dictionary, using predictive text, and more.

- Touch and hold text to highlight it, and then select from the following options:

  - I🔲 **Select all**: Highlights all the text in the field.

  - ✂ **Cut**: Removes the selected text and saves it to the clipboard.

  - 📋 **Copy**: Copies the selected text to the clipboard.

  - 📋 **Paste**: Insert the last copied or cut text into the current field.

  - 🔲 **Dictionary**: Access your personal dictionary.

Google Account

You will need a Google Account to access several phone features such as Gmail, Google Maps, Hangouts, and the Google Play applications. Before you are able to access Google applications, you must enter your account information. These applications sync between your phone and your online Google Account.

🔲 Google Account Cautions

Be sure not to forget your Google Account ID or password.

Create a Google Account

If you do not already have a Google Account, you can create one online or by using your phone.

Note: You can also create and sign into your Google/Gmail account through your phone's Setup application.

Note: Although you need a Gmail account to use certain features of your phone, such as Google Play, you do not need to use Gmail as the default account for your phone.

Create a Google Account Online

1. From a computer, launch a Web browser and navigate to google.com.

2. On the main page, click **Sign in**.

3. Click **Add account** > **Create an account**, and then follow the prompts to create your free account.

4. Look for an email from Google in the email inbox you provided, and respond to the email to confirm and activate your new account.

Create a Google Account Using Your Phone

1. From home, tap **Apps** ⊞ > **Settings** ⚙ > **Accounts** .

2. Tap **Add account**.

3. Tap **Google** > **Or create a new account**.

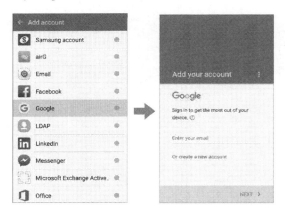

4. Enter your **First name** and **Last name**, and then tap **Next**.

5. Enter a desired **Username**, and then tap **Next**.

6. When prompted, enter and re-type a password. Then tap **Next**.

7. Enter a valid phone number to help you recover your Google Account and password if you ever forget it, and then tap **Next**. To skip this step, tap **Skip**.

Note: When setting up a new Google Account, either on your phone or online, you will be prompted to add a secondary email address. Enter a second Gmail address or any other email address from which you currently send and receive email. This address is used to authenticate your account should you ever encounter problems or forget your password. It is strongly encouraged for Android users so you can regain access to Google services and purchases on your phone.

8. Read the Google Terms of Service, Privacy Policy, and other legal documents, and then tap **I agree**.

9. Your phone connects with the Google servers and displays your account information. Tap **Next**.

10. Configure your Google data backup and communication, and then tap **Next**.

11. If desired, you can set up payment options for purchases through the Google Play store, and then tap **Next**.

❖ You are signed in to your new Google Account.

❖ Your Google Account is listed in **Apps**  > **Settings** > **Accounts** .

Sign In to Your Google Account

If you have a Google Account but have not yet signed in with your phone, follow these instructions to sign in to your Google Account.

1. From home, tap **Apps**  > **Settings** > **Accounts** .

2. Tap **Add account**.

3. Tap **Google**.

4. Tap Enter your email, enter your Gmail address, and then tap **Next**.

5. Enter your password and tap **Next**.

6. Read the Google Terms of Service, Privacy Policy, and other legal documents, and then tap **Accept**.

7. Configure your Google data backup and communication, and then tap **Next**.

8. Set up payment information for use in the Google Play store, and then tap **Next**.

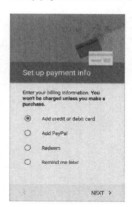

❖ You are now signed in to your Google Account, and your phone will start synchronizing with your Google Account.

❖ Your Google Account is listed in **Apps** ⊞ > **Settings** ◎ > **Accounts** ◉.

Note: Depending on your Google Account history, you may see a **Get your apps & data** screen instead of the **Sync your account** screen in step 8 above. Follow the prompts to complete your setup in either case.

Google Play Store

Google Play is the place to go to find new Android apps, books, movies, and music for your phone. Choose from a wide variety of free and paid content ranging from productivity apps and games to bestselling books and blockbuster movies and music. When you find what you want, you can easily download and install it on your phone.

To access the Google Play store app, you must first connect to the Internet using your phone's Wi-Fi or mobile data connection and sign in to your Google Account. See Browser and Sign In to Your Google Account for details.

Installing Applications

Many different kinds of applications can be installed on your phone from Google Play (provided by Google Inc.). Boost Mobile is not responsible in any way for user-installed applications (quality, reliability, legality, fitness for a purpose, credibility, accuracy, and more) or resulting malfunctions (viruses, and more).

Important: Our policies often do not apply to third-party applications. Third-party applications may access your personal information or require us to disclose your customer information to the third-party application provider. To find out how a third-party application will collect, access, use, or disclose your personal information, check the application provider's policies, which can usually be found on their website. If you aren't comfortable with the third-party application's policies, do not use the application.

Find and Install an App

When you install apps from Google Play app and use them on your phone, they may require access to your personal information (such as your location, contact data, and more) or access to certain functions or settings of your phone. Download and install only apps that you trust.

1. From home, tap **Apps** ⊞ > **Play Store** ▷.

2. When you open the Google Play store app for the first time, the Terms of Service window will appear. Tap **Accept** to continue.

3. Browse through the categories (**Apps & Games** or **Entertainment**), find an item you are interested in, and tap the name.

   - Browse through featured apps. Scroll through the list of featured apps when you open Google Play.

   - Search for an app. Tap the **Google Play** search field, enter the name or type of app you are looking for, and then tap 🔍 on the keyboard.

4. Tap an app to read a description about the app and user reviews.

5. Tap **Install** (for free applications) or the price (for paid applications).

Note: If you did not set up a payment option during phone setup or when adding your Google Account, you will be prompted to add a payment method when making a purchase from Google Play.

6. The subsequent screen notifies you whether the app will require access to your personal information or access to certain functions or settings of your phone. If you agree to the conditions, tap **Accept** (for free apps) or **Accept** and then **Buy** (for paid apps) to begin downloading and installing the app.

❖ The selected app is downloaded and installed on your phone.

Warning: Read the notification carefully! Be especially cautious with applications that have access to many functions or a significant amount of your data. Once you tap **OK** on this screen, you are responsible for the results of using this item on your phone.

▣ Purchasing Applications

Purchase apps at your own risk. Boost Mobile is not responsible for any disadvantage resulting for user or third parties.

Request a Refund for a Paid App

If you are not satisfied with an app, you can ask for a refund within 15 minutes of the purchase. Your credit card or other payment method is not charged and the app is uninstalled from your phone.

If you change your mind, you can install the app again, but you cannot request a refund a second time.

1. From home, tap **Apps** ⊞ > **Play Store** .

2. Tap **Menu** ☰ > **My apps**.

3. Tap the app to uninstall for a refund. The details screen for the app opens.

4. Tap **Refund**, and then tap **Yes** to confirm. Your app is uninstalled and the charge is cancelled.

Update an App

Depending on your settings, many apps will update automatically, or you can update apps directly from the Play store app.

Update an App Directly

1. From home, tap **Apps** ⊞ > **Play Store** .

2. Tap **Menu** ☰ > **My apps**.

3. Tap the app you want to update, and then tap **Update** > **Accept**.

❖ The app update is downloaded and installed.

Set Automatic App Updates

1. From home, tap **Apps** ⊞ > **Play Store** ▶.

2. Tap **Menu** ≡ > **My apps**.

3. Tap the app you want to set for auto-update, and then tap **More options** ⋮ > **Auto-update**.

❖ The app is set to update automatically whenever an update becomes available.

Note: Automatic updates are unavailable for some apps.

Uninstall an App

You can uninstall any app that you have downloaded and installed from the Google Play store.

1. From home, tap **Apps** ⊞ > **Play Store** ▶.

2. Tap **Menu** ≡ > **My apps**.

3. On the Installed screen, tap the app you want to uninstall, and then tap **Uninstall** > **OK**.

❖ The app is uninstalled and removed from your phone.

Get Help with Google Play

The Google Play store app offers an online help option if you have questions or want to know more about the app.

1. From home, tap **Apps** ⊞ > **Play Store** ▷.

2. Tap **Menu** ☰ > **Help & Feedback**.

❖ Your phone will display the Google Play store Help page, where you will find comprehensive, categorized information about Google Play. Tap **Browse all articles** to browse the full help menu, or tap **Search help** to search for specific topics.

Lock and Unlock Your Screen

Your phone allows you to quickly turn the screen off when not in use and to turn it back on and unlock it when you need it.

Turn the Screen Off When Not in Use

To quickly turn the screen off, press the **Power/Lock** key. Pressing the **Power/Lock** key again or receiving an incoming call will turn on your phone screen and show the lock screen.

—Power/Lock key

To save battery power, the phone automatically turns off the screen after a certain period of time when you leave it idle. You will still be able to receive messages and calls while the phone's screen is off.
Basic Operations

Note: For information on how to adjust the time before the screen turns off, see Display Settings.

Turn the Screen On and Unlock It

1. To turn the screen on, press the **Power/Lock** key.

—Power/Lock key

❖ The lock screen appears.

2. Swipe your finger across the screen to unlock it.

❖ The screen is unlocked.

▪ If you have set up a screen lock, you will be prompted to draw a pattern, enter a password, or enter a PIN. See Screen Lock.

Update Your Phone

From time to time, updates may become available for your phone. You can download and apply updates through the **Settings** > **System Update** menu.

Software Update Cautions

During update: The phone cannot be used until the software update is complete. It may take time to update your phone's software.

Signal during update: Update your phone where signal reception is good, and do not change location during the update process. Make sure the battery is adequately charged before beginning an update. A weak signal or low battery during an update may cause the update to fail. An update failure may disable the phone.

Other functions during update: Other phone functions cannot be used during a software update.

Update Your Phone Software

You can update your phone's software using the **System Update** option.

Before Updating Your Phone

Updating your phone may result in a loss of saved data depending on the condition of your phone (malfunctioning, damaged, water seepage, and more). You must back up all critical information before updating your phone firmware.

Back Up All Data Prior to Update

To back up your Gmail information:

1. From home, tap **Apps** ⊞ > **Settings** ⚙ > **Accounts** ◉ > **Google** > [your account].

2. Tap **ON/OFF** to enable backup of each item.

3. Tap **More** > **Sync now** to sync your Google Account information.

To back up your Exchange Mail information:

1. From home, tap **Apps** ⊞ > **Settings** ⚙ > **Accounts** ◉ > **Microsoft Exchange ActiveSync**.

2. Tap **ON/OFF** to enable backup of each option (Calendar, Contacts, Email, Tasks).

3. Tap **More** > **Sync now** to sync your Microsoft Exchange ActiveSync information.

Your Google app purchases are saved remotely and can be re-installed after the update is applied. To restore your Google apps following the update:

1. From home, tap **Apps** ⊞ > **Play Store** ▶.

2. Tap **Menu** ☰ > **My apps** > **All** tab.

3. Scroll through the list of previously downloaded Google apps and choose those you wish to reinstall.

4. Follow the prompts.

Update Your Phone's Software

Once you have backed up all your data, use the **Update now** option to update your phone's software.

- From home, tap **Apps** ⊞ > **Settings** ⚙ > **System Update** ◎ > **Update now**.

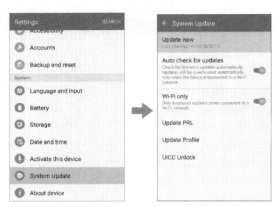

❖ Your phone automatically downloads and installs any available updates. You may be required to power your phone off and back on to complete the software update.

– or –

1. Locate the **System Update Available** icon ⬜ in notifications.

2. Slide the status bar down.

3. Tap ⬜ to open the System Updates screen.

4. Tap **Download** and follow the prompts. The downloading icon ⬇ appears within the status bar to indicate the phone is downloading the necessary files.

5. Follow the prompts to install the update and restart your phone.

Confirm Your Current Phone Software

1. From home, tap **Apps** ⦿ > **Settings** ⦿ > **About device** ⓘ.

2. Locate the Software version read-only field.

Update Your Profile

This option allows you to automatically update your online user profile information. If you choose to change your user name and select a new one online, you must then update the user name on your phone.

1. From home, tap **Apps** ⊞ > **Settings** ⚙ > **System Update** ⊘ > **Update Profile**.

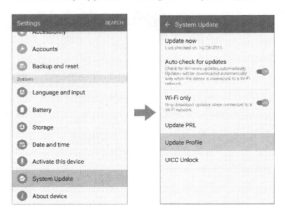

2. Follow the prompts.

   ❖ The phone will download and install the profile update and you will see a confirmation when complete.

Note: If your data services or account syncing ever seems to go out unexpectedly, use this feature to reconnect with the network.

Update Your PRL

This option allows you to download and update the PRL (preferred roaming list) automatically.

1. From home, tap **Apps** ⊞ > **Settings** ⚙ > **System Update** ⊘ > **Update PRL**.

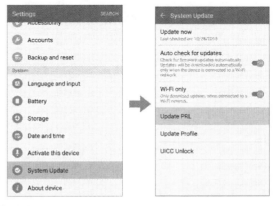

2. Follow the prompts.

   ❖ The phone will download and install the PRL update and you will see a confirmation when complete.

Your Phone Interface

The following topics describe how to use and customize your phone's home screen, understand the status bar, and use the notification panel.

Home Screen Basics

The home screen is the starting point for your phone's applications, functions, and menus. You can customize your home screen by adding application icons, shortcuts, folders, widgets, and more.

Home Screen Layout

Your home screen extends beyond the initial screen. Swipe the screen left or right to display additional screens.

Item	Description
Status area	The status area of the status bar (on the right) displays phone and service status information such as signal strength, battery status, Wi-Fi and data connectivity, ringer status, and time.

Item	Description
Status bar	The status bar displays icons to notify you of your phone's status (on the right side) and notifications (on the left side).
Widget	Widgets are self-contained apps that reside on your phone's home screen.
Application icons	Application icons are shortcuts to favorite applications. You can add and remove these shortcuts as you wish.
Applications (apps) list	Tap to open the applications (apps) list. The apps list key is a primary shortcut available from all home screens.
Primary shortcuts	Primary shortcuts are application shortcuts that appear in the same location on all of your phone's home screens. These are customizable except for the Applications (Apps) shortcut, which remains static.
Notification area	The notification area of the status bar (on the left) displays notifications for incoming messages, missed calls, application updates, and more.

Note: The indicator above the primary shortcuts lets you know your current screen position.

Tip: Press the Home key to return to the main home screen from any other screen.

Extended Home Screens

In addition to the main home screen, your phone features extended home screens to provide more space for adding icons, widgets, and more. Press the Home key to display the main home screen and then drag across the screen to move from the main screen to an extended screen.

- Swipe left or right to go to an extended home screen.
- While on an extended screen, press the Home key to return to the main home screen.

Add Home Screens

If you want to set up more shortcuts or widgets than you have space for, you can add more home screens.

1. Touch and hold an empty area on a home screen.

2. Scroll through the thumbnail screens to the right until you see a blank screen with a + sign.

3. Tap ✛ to add the screen.

❖ A new blank home screen will be added to the far right of your screens.

Status Bar and Notification Panel

Your phone's status and notifications are available at a glance at the top of the screen.

Status Bar

The status bar at the top of the home screen provides phone and service status information on the right side and notification alerts on the left. To view the notification panel or access the Quick settings menu, tap the status bar and drag it down.

Status Bar Layout

Notification area   Status area

Status bar

Main Status Icons

Icon	Status
✳	**Bluetooth active**: Bluetooth is active.
◉	**GPS active**: GPS is active.
📶	**Wi-Fi active**: Wi-Fi is active.
⬇	**Downloading**: A download is in progress.
📵	**Mute mode**: Mute mode is activated.
📳	**Vibrate mode**: Vibrate mode is activated.
📞	**Speakerphone**: Speakerphone is activated.
◢	**Network (strength)**: Network is at full signal.
ᴿ◢	**Network (roaming)**: A roaming network is currently being used.
³ᴳ◢	**3G data service**: The device is connected to a 3G wireless network.

Icon	Status
LTE	**4G LTE**: The device is connected to a 4G LTE wireless network.
	Airplane mode: Airplane mode is enabled.
	Sync active: Accounts are being synced.
	Battery (charging): The battery is charging.
	Battery (full charge): The battery is fully charged.

Main Notification Icons

Icon	Notification
	Missed call: A call has been missed.
	Call on hold: A call is on hold.
	New voicemail: New voicemail is available.
	New email: New email has arrived.
	New Gmail: New Gmail has arrived.
	New text or MMS message: New text or MMS messages have arrived.
	New Hangout message: A new Hangout message has arrived.
	New Boost Zone message: A new Boost Zone message has arrived.
	Event: An event is upcoming.
	USB connection: A USB connection is active.
	Alarm: An alarm is upcoming.
	Warning: A system alert has occurred.
	Update available: An update is available.

Icon	Notification
⬇	**Update downloading**: An update is currently downloading.
🗹	**Update successful**: An update has installed successfully.
⌨	**Keyboard active**: A keyboard is active.
⬤	**More notifications available**: Additional notifications are available. Drag down to view.

Notification Panel

Your phone's notifications appear at the left side of the status bar, and you can access the full notification panel by pulling down the status bar. From there, you can check notifications, download updates, open messaging apps, use the Quick settings menu, and more.

Open the Notification Panel

- Slide the status bar down. Slide your finger down from the top of the screen.

- ❖ The notification panel opens. To check notifications, tap an item in the list.

Close the Notification Panel

- Slide the notification panel up. (Slide your finger up from the bottom of the screen.)

  – or –

  Tap the **Back** key ⬑ to close the notification panel.

Notification Panel Layout

The notification panel gives you access to notifications, Settings, and the Quick settings menu.

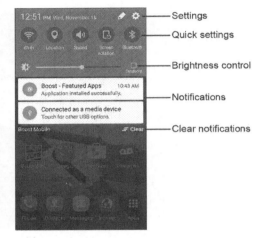 Settings

Quick settings

Brightness control

Notifications

Clear notifications

Notification Panel Quick Settings

The Quick settings list at the top of the notification panel lets you quickly access frequently used settings options. Scroll left or right to display all available settings, and tap an icon to turn the selected feature on or off.

You can customize which settings are available in your Quick settings list.

1. From a home screen, drag the status bar down to display the notification panel.

2. Tap **Edit** 🖉 to display the Quick settings panel options.

3. Drag buttons to arrange which options appear in the Quick settings panel.

  ▪ You will see two sets of buttons, Active buttons on top and Available buttons below.

    • You can have ten buttons active in the Quick settings panel. These appear in the Active buttons list.

    • There are additional buttons shown in the Available buttons list. These are not currently active in the Quick settings panel.

  ▪ To add, remove, or move a button, touch and hold it and move it to the desired location.

4. Tap **Done** when you are finished.

Note: You can only move buttons from Active to Available or vice-versa if there is space in the destination area. For example, if there are already ten Active buttons, you will need to move one to Available before dragging a different Available button up to the Active area.

Customize the Home Screen

Learn how to set the wallpaper and add, move, or remove shortcuts, widgets, and folders from the home screen.

Options for Rearranging the Home Screen

  • **Moving Widgets and Icons**: From home, touch and hold an item and then drag it to the desired location.

  • **Deleting Widgets and Icons**: From home, touch and hold an item and then drag it to **Remove** 🗑.

- **Displaying the Home Screen Menu**: From home, touch and hold an empty space to display the Home screen menu. Menu options include **Wallpapers**, **Widgets**, and **Themes**.

Change the Wallpaper

Select and assign your phone's background wallpaper.

1. From home, touch and hold an empty space, and then tap **Wallpapers** ▲.

- You can also access the Wallpaper menu through settings. From home, tap **Apps** ⚏ > **Settings** ⚙ > **Wallpaper** 🖼.

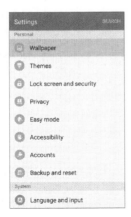

2. Tap **Home screen**, and then tap an option to select the wallpaper.

- **Home screen**: Set the background wallpaper for your home screen.

- **Lock screen**: Set the wallpaper for your phone's lock screen.

- **Home and lock screens**: Set a wallpaper for both your home screen and your lock screen.

3. Select a wallpaper and tap **Set as wallpaper**.

   ❖ The wallpaper is set.

Add Shortcuts to the Home Screen

You can add shortcuts for quick access to favorite apps from the home screen.

1. From home, tap **Apps** .

   ❖ The Apps list opens.

2. Touch and hold an app icon.

   ❖ The icon will disengage and you will see thumbnails of your home screens.

3. Drag the icon to an empty location on one of the home screens.

   ❖ The shortcut is added to the home screen.

Add Widgets to the Home Screen

You can add widgets to your phone's home screen. Widgets are self-contained apps that display on a home screen. Unlike a shortcut, the widget works like as an application. There are all kinds of widgets, including links to a specific contact, Internet bookmarks, Gmail and email accounts, and many others.

1. From home, touch and hold an empty space, and then tap **Widgets** ▦.

2. Touch and hold a widget icon.

   ❖ The icon will disengage and you will see thumbnails of your home screens.

3. Drag the icon to an empty location on one of the home screens.

   ❖ The widget is added to the home screen.

Add Folders to the Home Screen

You can group home screen shortcuts into folders for convenient access.

1. From home, touch and hold a shortcut you want to place in a folder, and then drag it on top of another shortcut and release it.

2. Type a name for the folder and tap **Done**.

   ❖ A new folder is created.

3. To add more app shortcuts to the folder, touch and hold a shortcut and drag it on top of the new folder.

   ❖ The new shortcut is added to the folder.

Change Folder Names

Once you have added folders, you can change the name easily from the folder display.

1. From home, tap the folder to open it, and then tap the folder name.

2. Type a new name and then tap **Done**.

Change the Folder Color

You can change the color of a folder.

1. From home, tap the folder to open it.

2. Tap  and select a color.

Phone App

The following topics outline the use of your device's phone app to place and receive calls, use voicemail, set up and manage contacts, and more.

Place and Answer Calls

The following topics describe how to directly dial calls, how to answer incoming calls, and how to use the in-call screen options.

Adjust In-Call Volume

- **Adjusting Call Volume**: Press the **Volume** key up or down during the call.

Troubleshooting

Problem: Difficulty during call.

> **Solution 1**: It may not be possible to make a call properly in a noisy location.

> **Solution 2**: When calling using Speaker, check the call volume. Raising the call volume may make calling difficult.

Problem: Sound pops momentarily during a call.

> **Solution**: Are you changing location while calling? Sound pops when signal is weak and the phone switches to a different area.

Call Using the Phone Dialer

The most "traditional" way to place a call is by using the phone's dialer screen.

1. From home, tap **Phone**  to display the phone screen.

   ❖ The phone app opens. If necessary, tap  to display the keypad.

2. Tap the number keys on the keypad to enter the phone number.

   ▪ As you enter digits, Smart Dial searches for contacts that match. If you see the number you want to dial, tap the contact to fill in the number on the keypad.

3. Tap  to call the number.

 * The phone dials the number. The call begins when the other party answers.

4. To end the call, tap ⬇.

 * The call ends.

Troubleshooting

Problem: Call does not connect.

   Solution 1: Was the number dialed using the correct area code?

   Solution 2: Are you in an area with poor wireless coverage? Try calling again from another area.

Call Emergency Numbers

You can place calls to 9-1-1 even if the phone's screen is locked or your account is restricted.

To call the 9-1-1 emergency number when the phone's screen is locked with a screen lock:

1. From the lock screen, swipe the Phone shortcut 📞 up, and then tap **Emergency call**.

2. Tap ⟨9⟩ ⟨1⟩ ⟨1⟩ 📞.

 * As long as you are in an area covered by wireless service, the emergency call is placed.

To call the 9-1-1 emergency number normally or when your account is restricted:

1. Unlock the screen. For more information, see Lock and Unlock Your Screen.

2. From home, tap **Phone** 📞.

- If necessary, tap 🔘 to display the keypad.

3. Tap ⌗9⌗ ⌗1⌗ ⌗1⌗ 📞.

   ❖ As long as you are in an area covered by wireless service, the emergency call is placed.

Enhanced 9-1-1 (E 9-1-1) Information

This phone features an embedded Global Positioning System (GPS) chip necessary for utilizing E 9-1-1 emergency location services where available.

When you place an emergency 9-1-1 call, the GPS feature of your phone seeks information to calculate your approximate location. Depending on several variables, including availability and access to satellite signals, it may take up to 30 seconds or more to determine and report your approximate location.

Important: Always report your location to the 9-1-1 operator when placing an emergency call. Some designated emergency call takers, known as Public Safety Answering Points (PSAPs), may not be equipped to receive GPS location information from your phone.

Answer Phone Calls

The following information lets you know how to answer incoming calls, mute the ringer on incoming calls, reject incoming calls, and more.

When you receive a phone call from a contact, the Incoming call screen appears and displays the caller ID icon, name, and phone number of the calling party. When you receive a phone call from someone who is not stored in Contacts, only the default caller ID icon and phone number appear on the Incoming call screen.

Note: If your phone is turned off, all calls automatically go to voicemail.

Answer an Incoming Call

1. When a call arrives, drag 📞 to the right to answer it.

   ❖ The call begins.

2. To end the call, tap 📞.

   ❖ The call ends.

Mute the Ringing Sound

- To mute the ringer without rejecting the call, press the **Volume** key down.

Reject an Incoming Call

■ When a call arrives, drag  to the left to reject it.

❖ The ringtone or vibration will stop and call will be sent directly to voicemail.

Reject a Call and Send a Text Message

You can reject an incoming call and automatically send a text message to the caller.

1. When a call arrives, drag **Reject call with message** up from the bottom of the screen.

2. Tap one of the messages to send it to the caller.

❖ The selected message will be delivered to the caller.

- You can edit existing reject messages or create new ones through the Call settings menu. From home, tap **Phone**  > **More** > **Settings** > **Call blocking** > **Call-reject messages** and edit or create reject messages.

In-Call Screen Layout and Options

While you are on a call, you will see a number of options.

In-Call Screen Layout

Tap options to activate them during a call.

- ✛ **Add call**: Tap to initiate a conference call.

  - After the second call is placed, tap ⟩⟶ **Merge** to join the two calls (conference).

- 📞 **Extra volume**: Increase the current volume of the call.

- ✳ **Bluetooth**: Route the phone's audio through a connected Bluetooth headset (On) or through the speaker (Off).

  - When the call is routed to a Bluetooth headset, the current call area shows the Bluetooth 📶 icon.

Note: The Bluetooth button is activated to show the current call is routed to the connected Bluetooth headset.

  - To route the current call back to the phone, tap **Bluetooth** ✳ to temporarily use the phone. Tap it again to route the call back to the connected Bluetooth headset.

  - When Bluetooth or the Bluetooth headset is turned off, the call is routed through either the earpiece or speaker.

- ◀)) **Speaker**: Route the phone's audio through the speaker (On) or through the earpiece (Off).

  - Activate **Speaker** to route the phone's audio through the speaker. (You can adjust the speaker volume using the **Volume** key.)

  - Deactivate **Speaker** to use the phone's earpiece.

Warning: Because of higher volume levels, do not place the phone near your ear during speakerphone use.

- ⠿ **Keypad/Hide**: Toggle the appearance of the keypad.

- 🎙 **Mute**: Mute the microphone during an active call. Tap again to unmute the microphone.

Note: If Mute is activated, the speaker mode is deactivated.

- **End call**: Tap 🔴 to end the current call.

Additional In-Call Options

- Swipe left to display additional in-call options:

  - **Email**: Send an email while remaining on the call.

  - **Message**: Send a text or multimedia message while remaining on the call.

  - **Internet**: Launch a Web browser while remaining on the call.

  - **Contacts**: Display your Contacts list while remaining on the call.

  - **Calendar**: View your calendar while remaining on the call.

  - **Memo**: Create a new memo while remaining on the call.

End of Call Options

When a call ends, you will briefly see an end-of-call options screen, which may include:

- **View contact**: Display the contact information for the caller.

- **Create contact**: Create a new contact entry for the caller. See Add a Contact.

- **Update existing**: Add the caller's phone number to an existing contact entry. See Edit a Contact.

- **Add event**: Schedule a meeting and invite the caller. See Add an Event to the Calendar.

- **Call**: Place a call to the caller.

- **Message**: Address a text message to the caller. See Send a Text Message.

Place a Call from Contacts

You can place phone calls directly from entries in your Contacts list.

1. From home, tap **Phone** .

2. Tap **Contacts** to display the Contacts list.

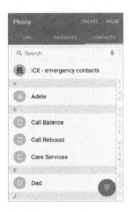

❖ The Contacts list appears.

3. Tap a contact.

4. Tap **Call** 📞 next to the number you want to call.

   ❖ The phone dials the number. The call begins when the other party answers.

5. To end the call, tap 📞.

Tip: You can also place a call directly from the Contacts list. Swipe the entry you want to call from left to right to place a call to the entry's primary number.

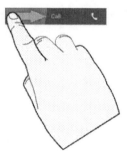

Call from Call Logs

The call logs list lets you quickly place calls to recent incoming, outgoing, or missed numbers.

1. From home, tap **Phone** .

2. Tap **Log** to display the call logs list.

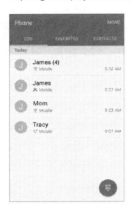

❖ The call logs list appears.

3. Tap an entry to display the call details.

4. Tap 📞 to place a call.

   ❖ The phone dials the number. The call begins when the other party answers.

   ▪ For additional options, tap the name or number.

5. To end the call, tap ⬤.

Tip: You can also place a call directly from the Call logs list. Swipe the entry you want to call from left to right to place a call.

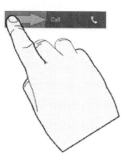

Optional Services

The following topics outline additional voice-related services available with your phone, including call services, voicemail, and more.

Voicemail Setup

You should set up your voicemail and personal greeting as soon as your phone is activated. Always use a password to protect against unauthorized access. Your phone automatically transfers all unanswered calls to your voicemail, even if your phone is in use or turned off.

1. From home, tap **Phone** 📞 to display the phone screen.

   ❖ The phone app opens. If necessary, tap 🔘 to display the keypad.

2. Touch and hold ⎣ 1 ⎦ to dial your voicemail number.

   ❖ Your phone dials the voicemail access number.

3. Follow the system prompts to:

   ▪ Create your password.

   ▪ Record your name announcement.

   ▪ Record your greeting.

Important: Voicemail Password – It is strongly recommended that you create a password when setting up your voicemail to protect against unauthorized access. Without a password, anyone who has access to your phone is able to access your voicemail messages.

Visual Voicemail

Visual Voicemail gives you a quick and easy way to access your voicemail. Now you can find exactly the message you are looking for without having to listen to every voicemail message first. This feature periodically goes out to your voicemail, and gathers the caller information from all of the current voicemails. It then populates a list with the caller name and number, along with the length of time and priority level of the voicemail message.

Set Up Visual Voicemail

Setting up Visual Voicemail follows many of the same procedures as setting up traditional voicemail. You should set up your voicemail and personal greeting as soon as your phone is activated. Your phone automatically transfers all unanswered calls to your voicemail, even if your phone is in use or turned off.

Note: To set up your traditional voicemail box, see Voicemail Setup.

1. From home, tap **Apps** ⊞ > **Voicemail** 🔘.

   – or –

   Tap **Phone** 📞, and then tap 🔘 to access your Visual Voicemail.

2. Scroll through the Welcome to Visual Voicemail introduction screens to view a brief explanation of the visual voicemail services.

3. At the end of the welcome screens, a Personalize your voicemail prompt displays.

❖ You will see a Personalize your voicemail prompt.

4. Tap **Personalize now** and follow the system prompts to:

- Create a password (part of standard voicemail).

- Record your name announcement.

- Record your greeting.

Important: Voicemail Password – It is strongly recommended that you create a password when setting up your voicemail to protect against unauthorized access. Without a password, anyone who has access to your phone is able to access your voicemail messages.

Review Visual Voicemail

Visual Voicemail lets you easily access and select which messages you want to review.

1. From home, tap **Apps** ⊞ > **Voicemail** .

❖ You will see the voicemail inbox.

2. Tap a message, and then tap **Play** ▶ to review it.

Tip: There are several icons at the bottom of the review screen for maintenance, storage, messaging, and other options. For an explanation of all your options, tap **More options** ⋮ > **Help** > **Visual Voicemail Menu** > **Visual Voicemail Settings**.

Listen to Multiple Voicemail Messages

When you are done listening to a voicemail message you can easily access other voicemail messages without returning to the main voicemail screen.

1. Listen to the current voicemail message.

2. Swipe your finger left or right to display the next or previous message.

You can navigate through voicemail messages as frequently as you would like. You can even move to the next or previous message before you are finished listening to the current one.

Visual Voicemail Options

Your visual voicemail options appear as icons at the bottom of the voicemail review screen.

1. From home, tap **Apps** ▦ > **Voicemail** ▣.

2. The following options are available when viewing new voicemail messages:

   - **Subscribe**: Subscribe to the premium Voice-to-Text transcription service. (This service requires an additional monthly charge.)

   - **Play all new**: Play all new messages.

   - **Select multiple**: Perform an action on multiple messages.

   - **Compose Avatar message**: Send an animated voice message to friends. You can also compose an Avatar message by tapping ▣.

   - **More options**: Access Search, Settings, and Help features.

3. Tap a message to review it. The following options are available while listening to voicemail messages:

   - **Call**: Dial the number the message came from.

   - **Share**: Send the message using Wi-Fi Direct, social accounts, and more.

   - **Delete**: Delete selected messages.

Phone App   79

- ◂ **Reply**: Reply to the message using text or voice message.

- ⋮ **More options**: Access Archive, Settings, and Help features.

4. Touch and hold a message to manage your messages. The following options are available:

   - ▢ **All**: Select all messages.

   - 🗑 **Delete**: Delete the selected messages.

   - 💾 **Archive**: Save this message.

   - ✉ **Mark as Read**: Mark this voicemail as being read.

   - ✉ **Mark as Unread**: Mark this voicemail as not being read.

Note: Not all options are available for all messages.

Configure Visual Voicemail Settings

The Visual Voicemail settings menu lets you access settings for notifications, pictures, greetings, and more.

1. From home, tap **Apps** ⊞ > **Voicemail** 🔘.

2. Tap **More options** ⋮ > **Settings**.

❖ You will see the voicemail settings menu.

3. Select an option to change its settings:

- **Avatar**: Configure you Avatar options.

- **Display**: Change your voicemail message theme and enter a name to identify yourself to people when replying or forwarding messages.

- **Help**: View help topics for using Visual Voicemail.

- **Preferences**: Change your Visual Voicemail application preferences.

- **Sound**: Change your sound/speakerphone options.

- **Updates**: Check for updates.

- **About Voicemail**: View information about the application.

Change Your Main Greeting Using the Voicemail Menu

Your main greeting can be changed directly using the Visual Voicemail system. This direct access saves you from having to navigate within the voicemail menu.

1. From home, tap **Apps**  > **Voicemail** .

2. Tap **More options** ⋮ > **Settings** > **Preferences** > **Personalize voicemail**.

3. Tap **OK** to connect to the voicemail system. Follow the prompts to change your current greeting.

Edit the Display Name Using the Voicemail Menu

From your Visual Voicemail menu, you can quickly change the name or number attached to your voice messages.

1. From home, tap **Apps**  > **Voicemail** .

2. Tap **More options** ⋮ > **Settings** > **Display** > **Display name**.

3. Tap the existing identification field and enter a new identifying name or number (used to identify you to recipients of your voice messages).

4. Tap **OK** to save your information.

Caller ID Blocking

Caller ID identifies a caller before you answer the phone by displaying the number of the incoming call. If you do not want your number displayed when you make a call, follow these steps.

1. From home, tap **Phone** 📞 to display the phone screen.

❖ The phone app opens. If necessary, tap 🔵 to display the keypad.

2. Tap `*` `6` `7`.

3. Enter a phone number.

4. Tap 📞.

❖ Your caller information will not appear on the recipient's phone.

To permanently block your number, call Boost Customer Service.

Call Waiting

When you are on a call, Call Waiting alerts you to incoming calls by sounding a long beep. Your phone's screen informs you that another call is coming in and displays the caller's phone number (if it is available).

To respond to an incoming call while you are on a call:

- Slide  to the right. (This puts the first caller on hold and answers the second call.)

To switch back to the first caller:

- Tap **Swap** ⬒.

Conference Calling

With conference calling, also known as 3-way calling, you can talk to two people at the same time. When using this feature, the normal airtime rates will be charged for each of the two calls.

1. From home, tap **Phone** 📞 to display the phone screen.

❖ The phone app opens. If necessary, tap 🔵 to display the keypad.

2. Once you have established the connection, tap **Add call**, and dial the second number (or place the call from Log or Contacts).

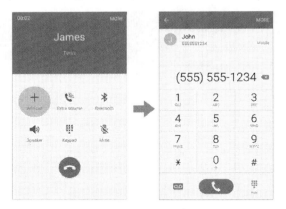

❖ This puts the first caller on hold and dials the second number.

3. When you are connected to the second party, tap **Merge** ⊃⤳. Your conference call is now in session.

4. To end the three-way call, tap ●.

Note: If one of the people you called hangs up during your call, you and the remaining caller stay connected. If you initiated the call and are the first to hang up, all callers are disconnected.

Call Forwarding

Call Forwarding lets you forward all your incoming calls to another phone number – even when your phone is turned off. You can continue to make calls from your phone when you have activated Call Forwarding.

Note: You are charged a higher rate for calls you have forwarded.

To activate Call Forwarding:

1. From home, tap **Phone** 📞 to display the phone screen.

   ❖ The phone app opens. If necessary, tap 🔵 to display the keypad.

2. Tap ⬚ * ⬚ 7 ⬚ 2 ⬚.

3. Enter the area code and phone number to which you want your calls forwarded.

4. Tap 📞.

   ❖ You will hear a tone to confirm the activation of Call Forwarding. All calls to your wireless number will be forwarded to the designated phone number.

To deactivate Call Forwarding:

1. From home, tap **Phone** .

   ❖ The phone app opens. If necessary, tap 🔘 to display the keypad.

2. Tap ⟦ * ⟧ ⟦ 7 ⟧ ⟦ 2 ⟧ ⟦ 0 ⟧.

3. Tap 📞.

   ❖ You will hear a tone to confirm the deactivation.

Phone Settings

Configure options for calling with your phone.

Tip: You can also access Phone settings from the Phone app. From home, tap **Phone** 📞 > **More** > **Settings**.

1. From home, tap **Phone**  to display the phone screen.

❖ The phone app opens. If necessary, tap 🔘 to display the keypad.

2. Tap **More** > **Settings** to configure options:

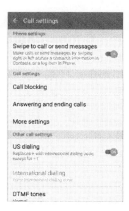

- **Swipe to call or send messages**: Make calls or send messages by swiping right or left across a contact's information in Contacts, or a log item in the Phone app.

- **Call blocking**: Create and manage a list of phone numbers, to have your phone automatically block calls you receive from those numbers, and compose or edit response messages when rejecting incoming calls.

  - **Block list**: Enter telephone numbers to block calls from the numbers when Call blocking is turned on.

- **Call-reject messages**: Create and manage text messages to send to callers when rejecting incoming calls. Messages you create here are available from the incoming call screen when you use the Reject with message option.

- **Answering and ending calls**: Manage settings for answering and ending calls.

  - **Pressing the Home key**: Answer calls by pressing the **Home** key.

  - **Pressing the Power key**: End calls by pressing the **Power/Lock** key.

- **More settings**: Settings for TTY and Hearing Aids are located in this option.

  - **TTY mode**: A TTY (teletypewriter, also known as a TDD or Text Telephone) is a telecommunications device that allows people who are deaf, hard of hearing, or who have speech or language disabilities, to communicate by telephone. Your phone is compatible with select TTY phones. Please check with the manufacturer of your TTY device to ensure that it supports digital wireless transmission. Your phone and TTY device will connect using a special cable that plugs into your phone's headset jack. If this cable was not provided with your TTY device, contact your TTY device manufacturer to purchase the connector cable.

  - **Hearing aids**: Improve the sound quality for use with hearing aids.

- **US dialing**: Replace "+" with the international access code for your location.

- **International dialing**: Use the International dialing code to replace "+".

- **DTMF tones**: Set the length of Dual-tone Multi-frequency (DTMF) tones which play when you use the keypad during a call, such as when navigating menus.

- **Voicemail settings**: Set options for Visual Voicemail. See Configure Visual Voicemail Settings.

Access Call Settings

- From home, tap **Phone**  > **More** > **Settings**.

- ❖ The Call settings menu displays.

Call Settings Options

Use the Call settings menu to adjust the following settings:

Setting	Description
Swipe to call or send messages	Place a call to a displayed contact by swiping right. Send a message to a displayed contact by swiping left.
Call blocking	Manage a list of automatically blocked phone numbers, and create or edit messages to block incoming calls.
Answering and ending calls	Answer calls by pressing the **Home** key. End calls by pressing the **Power/Lock** key.
More settings	**TTY mode**: Enable service on your phone. **Hearing aids**: Improve the sound quality of your phone when using hearing aids.
US dialing	Replace + with the international dialing code, except when entering +1.
International dialing	Enter the international dialing code automatically (only when US dialing is disabled).

Setting	Description
DTMF tones	Set the length of DTMF tones, which are used when pressing the keypad while on a call.
Voicemail settings	Configure your voicemail.

Contacts

The Contacts application lets you store and manage contacts from a variety of sources, including contacts you enter and save directly in your phone as well as contacts synchronized with your Google Account, your PC, compatible email programs (including Exchange Server), and your Facebook friends.

⚙ Contacts Cautions

Information saved in Contacts may be lost or changed if the battery is left uncharged. Accident or malfunction may also cause loss or change to information. It is recommended that you keep a separate copy of contacts and other important information. Boost Mobile is not responsible for any damages from lost or changed contacts.

Contacts Screen Layout

The following illustration show's your Contacts app layout and describes the various features.

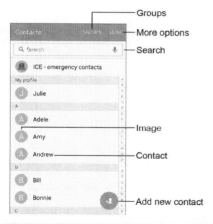

Groups

More options

Search

Image

Contact

Add new contact

Item	Description
Groups	Show contact groups.
More options	Access additional options.
Search	Search contacts.
Image	Show the contact's photo.

Item	Description
Contact	Show the contact's details.
Add new contact	Add a new contact.

Add a Contact

You can add contacts from the Contacts application. Enter details such as name, phone numbers, email addresses, mailing addresses, and more.

1. From home, tap **Apps** ⊞ > **Contacts** .

❖ You will see the Contacts list.

2. Tap  to add a contact.

❖ The Save contact to screen appears.

3. If you have multiple account types associated with your phone, select a contact type.

- Select **Device** as the sync account if you want your contacts on your phone only; they will not be synced with your Google Account.

- Select **Google** if you want to save contacts to your Google Account; these will be synced automatically with your Google Account online. If you have multiple Google Accounts set up, you will need to pick a specific account.

- Select **Microsoft Exchange ActiveSync** to sync your contacts automatically with your Microsoft Exchange account.

Note: If you do not see the Save contact to screen and you have multiple accounts set up, you can select an account by tapping the account type in the upper left corner.

4. Use the keyboard to enter as much information as you want.

- **Photo**: Tap  to assign a picture to the contact.

- **Name**: Enter the contact's name.

- **Phone number**: Enter a phone number for the contact.

- **Email**: Enter an email address.

- **Groups**: If desired, assign the contact to one or more contact groups.

- **Add another field**: Add additional information, such as Organization, Address, Web address, IM account, Event (e.g., birthday), Notes, Nickname, Phonetic name, Relationship, Ringtone, Message tone, and Vibration pattern.

Note: To select a type (label) for a phone number, email address, or address (such as Mobile, Home, Work, and more), tap the type to the right of the field and select the appropriate type.

Note: To add more phone numbers, email addresses, and more, tap ✛ on the right side of the entry field.

5. When you have finished adding information, tap **Save**.

❖ The contact is added.

Save a Phone Number

You can save a phone number to Contacts directly from the phone keypad.

1. From home, tap **Phone** 📞 to display the phone screen.

❖ The phone app opens. If necessary, tap ⚫ to display the keypad.

2. Enter a phone number and tap ✛ **Add to Contacts**.

3. To add a new contact, tap **Create contact**. To add the number to an existing contact, tap **Update existing**.

   ▪ For an existing contact, tap the contact name and select a number type for the new number.

   ▪ For a new contact, enter the name and any additional information.

4. Tap **Save**.

   ❖ The contact is added.

View Contacts

View a contact's details by displaying a contact entry.

1. From home, tap **Apps** ⊞ > **Contacts** ⬆.

❖ You will see the Contacts list.

2. Tap a contact to view its details.

❖ The contact's detailed listing appears.

Edit a Contact

Once you have added a contact, you can add or edit any of the information in the entry, assign a caller ID picture, customize with a unique ringtone, and more.

1. From home, tap **Apps**  > **Contacts** .

   ❖ You will see the Contacts list.

2. Tap a contact to view its details.

   ❖ The contact's detailed listing appears.

3. Tap **Edit.**

4. Tap any field you want to change or add. See Add a Contact.

5. Add or edit the information, and then tap **Save**.

❖ Your changes are saved to the contact entry.

Delete a Contact

You can delete a contact from the contacts details page.

1. From home, tap **Apps** ⊞ > **Contacts** 📇.

❖ You will see the Contacts list.

2. Tap a contact to view its details.

❖ The contact's detailed listing appears.

3. Tap **More** > **Delete** > **Delete**.

❖ The contact is deleted.

Tip: You can also touch and hold the contact from the Contacts list and tap **Delete** > **Delete**.

Share a Contact

You can quickly share contacts using Bluetooth, email, Gmail, or text messaging.

1. From home, tap **Apps** ⊞ > **Contacts** ⬤.

Contacts

❖ You will see the Contacts list.

2. Tap a contact to display it, and then tap **More** > **Share contact**.

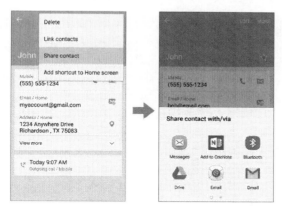

❖ You will see list of sharing methods.

3. Select a sharing method:

- **Add to OneNote**: Save the information to your OneNote account.

- **Bluetooth**: Send the information using Bluetooth. See Bluetooth for information on pairing and sending using Bluetooth.

- **Drive**: Save the information to your Google Drive account.

- **Email**: Send the information as an email attachment. See Compose and Send Email.

- **Gmail**: Send the information as a Gmail attachment. See Create and Send a Gmail Message.

- **Messages**: Send the information in a text message. See Send a Multimedia Message (MMS).

- **OneDrive**: Save the information to your OneDrive account.

- **Wi-Fi Direct**: Send the information to another device using Wi-Fi Direct. See Wi-Fi Direct.

4. Complete the required steps as prompted for the selected method.

❖ The selected contact will be shared.

Import Contacts

Import (load) contacts that have been backed up to device storage.

Import Contacts from Device Storage

1. From home, tap **Apps**  > **Contacts** .

   ❖ You will see the Contacts list.

2. Tap **More** > **Settings** > **Import/Export contacts**.

   ❖ You will see the Import/Export contacts menu.

3. Tap **Import**.

4. Select a destination for the imported contacts.

5. Follow the prompts to complete the import.

   ❖ The contacts are imported and stored in the selected account.

Back Up Contacts

If you are saving contacts to an account that does not automatically back them up using the Cloud, you can manually back them up to your phone's memory for re-import if needed.

1. From home, tap **Apps** ⊞ > **Contacts** 🔽.

 ❖ You will see the Contacts list.

2. Tap **More** > **Settings** > **Import/Export contacts**.

 ❖ You will see the Import/Export contacts menu.

3. Tap **Export**.

 ❖ The contacts are exported.

Contacts Settings

Configure options for contacts stored on your phone.

1. From home, tap **Apps** ⬛ > **Contacts** 🔵.

 ❖ You will see the Contacts list.

2. Tap **More** > **Settings** to configure options:

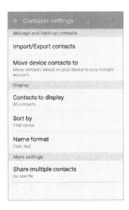

- **Import/Export contacts**: Import contacts from your phone's internal memory and export contacts to your phone's internal memory.

- **Move device contacts to**: Move contacts saved on your device to your Google or Samsung accounts.

- **Contacts to display**: Choose contacts to display in Contacts. You can choose only contacts from your phone's memory, or from an account, or choose other sources. You can also create a customized list of contacts to display.

- **Sort by**: Choose how contacts are sorted, by first or last name.

- **Name format**: Choose how contacts are displayed, by first or last name.

- **Share multiple contacts**: You can choose how to transfer contacts, when sharing them with other devices, using sharing methods such as Bluetooth.

    - **As one file**: Multiple contacts are sent together. This method can be faster, but depends on whether the target device can accept multiple name cards. If not, only one contact will be sent.

    - **Individually**: Name cards are sent individually. This method may take longer, because the other device must accept each name card individually, but it helps ensure that no name cards are missed.

Messaging and Internet

With wireless service and your phone's messaging and data capabilities, you have the opportunity to share information through many different channels and accounts, including Gmail (Google), personal and corporate email, text and multimedia messaging, social networking accounts, and Hangouts.

Text and Multimedia Messaging

With Text Messaging (SMS), you can send and receive instant text messages between your wireless phone and another messaging-ready phone.

Multimedia messages, or MMS, can contain text and pictures, recorded voice, audio or video files, picture slideshows, contact cards (vCard), or appointments (vCalendar).

See your service plan for applicable charges for messaging.

Send a Text Message

Quickly compose and send text messages on your phone.

1. From home, tap **Apps** ⊞ > **Messages** ▣.

2. On the Messaging screen, tap **Compose** ◉.

   ❖ The Compose screen opens.

3. Fill in one or more recipients. You can:

   ▪ Enter phone numbers directly in the **Enter recipients** field. If you are sending the message to several phone numbers, separate the phone numbers with a comma. As you enter information, any matching phone numbers from your Contacts list are displayed. Tap a match to enter that number or address directly.

- Tap **Recipients** , and then select the contacts to whom you want to send the message. You can also select contact groups as recipients. When you have selected all the message recipients, tap **Done**.

4. Tap the **Enter message** field and then start composing your message.

Tip: To add a subject line, tap **More** > **Message options** > **Add subject**.

5. When done, tap [SEND] to send the text message.

Send a Multimedia Message (MMS)

When you need to add a little more to a text message, you can send a multimedia message (MMS) with pictures, voice recordings, audio or video files, contact cards (vCard), or appointments (vCalendar).

1. From home, tap **Apps** ▦ > **Messages** ▣.

2. On the Messaging screen, tap **Compose** ✎.

   ❖ The Compose screen opens.

3. Fill in one or more recipients. You can:

   ▪ Enter phone numbers directly in the **Enter recipient** field. If you are sending the message to several phone numbers, separate the phone numbers with a comma. As you enter information, any matching phone numbers from your Contacts list are displayed. Tap a match to enter that number or address directly.

   ▪ Tap the 🖳 icon, and then select the contacts to whom you want to send the message. You can also select contact groups as recipients. When you have selected all the message recipients, tap **Done**.

4. Tap the **Enter message** field, and then start composing your message.

Tip: To add a subject line, tap **More** > **Message options** > **Add subject**.

5. Tap  and select from the following file attachments:

- **Image**: Attach a stored picture. See Gallery.

- **Take picture**: Take a new picture and attach it. See Camera and Video.

- **Video**: Attach a stored video. See Gallery.

- **Record video**: Record a new video and attach it. See Camera and Video.

- **Audio**: Attach a stored music file or voice recording.

- **Record audio**: Make a voice recording and attach it. See Voice Recorder.

- **Memo**: Attach a Memo. See Memo.

- **Calendar:** Select the calendar event you want to attach. See Calendar.

- **Maps:** Add your current location (requires GPS to be turned on) or a location you pick on a map to your message. See Google Maps.

- **Contacts:** Select a contact from your phone, and then select which contact information you want to attach. See Contacts.

6. To make changes to or remove your attachment, touch and hold the item.

7. Tap ▣ to send the MMS message.

Create a Slideshow

In a multimedia message, you can add slides, each containing a picture, video, or audio.

1. In the multimedia message you are composing, tap **More** > **Message options** > **Add slide** to add space for a new slide.

2. To compose your slideshow, do any of the following:

  - **Add a picture**: Tap  > **Image** and select a picture.

  - **Add a video**: Tap 📎 > **Video** and select a video. (You cannot add both a picture and a video on the same slide.)

  - **Add music or a voice recording**: Tap 📎 > **Audio** and select a file.

  - **Add a new slide**: Tap **More** > **Message options** > **Add slide**.

  - **Preview your slideshow**: Tap **More** > **Message options** > **Preview**.

  - For more options, tap **More** > **Message options** and select an option.

3. When you have finished composing the multimedia message, tap 🔲.

Tip: To compose a slide show, you can also simply attach multiple items separately to the MMS message. Tap 📎 and select a file type, location, and file and then repeat it for additional slides. Your phone will automatically compile a slide show.

Save and Resume a Draft Message

While composing a text or multimedia message, tap **Back** ⤴ to automatically save your message as a draft. Your message will display Draft on the main Messaging screen.

To resume composing the message:

1. From home, tap **Apps** ⦂ > **Messages** 📧.

2. Tap the message marked Draft to resume editing it.

3. When you finish editing the message, tap ▦.

New Messages Notification

Depending on your notification settings, the phone will play a ringtone, vibrate, or display the message briefly in the status bar when you receive a new text or multimedia message.

A new message icon ✉ also appears in the notifications area of the status bar to notify you of a new text or multimedia message. The Messages application icon also displays the number of new messages 🗨.

- To open the message, drag the status bar down to open the notification panel. Tap the new message to open and read it.

  – or –

  From home, tap **Apps** ⊞ > **Messages** 🗨, and then tap the conversation.

For information on reading and replying to messages see Manage Message Conversations.

Manage Message Conversations

Text and multimedia messages that are sent to and received from a contact (or a number) are grouped into conversations or message threads in the Messaging screen. Text or MMS conversations let you see exchanged messages (similar to a chat program) with a contact on the screen.

Read a Text Message

- Do one of the following:

  - On the Messaging screen, tap the text message or conversation to open and read it.

  - If you have a new message notification, drag the status bar down to open the notification panel. Tap the new message to open and read it.

To return to the Messaging screen from a conversation, tap **Back** ⤺.

Note: To view the details of a particular message, in the conversation, touch and hold the message to open the options menu, and then tap **View message details**.

Note: If a message contains a link to a Web page, tap the message and then tap the link to open it in the Web browser.

Note: If a message contains a phone number, tap the message and then tap the phone number to dial the number or add it to your contacts.

View a Multimedia Message (MMS)

1. From home, tap **Apps** ⊞ > **Messages** ⊠.

2. On the Messaging screen, tap a multimedia message or conversation to open it.

3. Tap the attachment to open it.

   ▪ If the attachment is a vCard contact, it is imported to your phone's Contacts list. For more information, see Contacts.

   ▪ If the attachment is a vCalendar file, you can choose the calendar where you want to save the event. For information on using Calendar, see Calendar.

   ▪ For other media (like photos or videos), you can choose where to save the attachment and which app to use to open it.

4. To save the attachment to device memory, touch and hold the attachment, and then tap **Save attachment**.

Note: When Auto retrieve in MMS settings is disabled, only the message header is downloaded. To download the entire message, tap the **Download** button in the message.

Note: If you are concerned about the size of your data downloads, check the multimedia message size before you download it.

Reply to a Message

1. From home, tap **Apps** 🎛 > **Messages** ⊠.

2. On the Messaging screen, tap a conversation to open it.

3. Tap the **Enter message** field at the bottom of the screen, enter your reply message, and then tap **Send** 🔲.

Note: To reply to a text message with a multimedia message, open the text message and tap ⌀. The text message is automatically converted into a multimedia message.

Delete Conversations

1. From home, tap **Apps** 🎛 > **Messages** ⊠.

2. On the Messaging screen, touch and hold a conversation to delete.

3. Select any additional conversations you want to delete, and then tap **Delete** > **Delete**.

Delete Message

1. While viewing a conversation, touch and hold a message.

2. Tap **Delete** > **Delete**.

View Contact Information from a Message

When you receive a message from someone in your stored contacts, you can tap the contact's picture or icon in the conversation to open a menu of options. Depending on the stored contact information, you can view the contact details, place a phone call or send an email message to the contact, and more.

Messages Settings

The messages settings menu lets you control options for your text and MMS messages including message limits, size settings, and notifications.

1. From home, tap **Apps** ⊞ > **Messages** ⬜.

2. Tap **More** > **Settings** to configure options:

- **Notifications**: When turned on, notifications for new messages display in the status bar. Tap **ON/OFF** to turn the setting on, and then configure options:

  - **Notification sound**: Choose a sound to play for new message notifications.

  - **Vibrations**: Choose whether vibration plays along with the sound for new message notifications.

- **Pop-up display**: Choose whether a new message pops up on the display to notify you.

- **Quick responses**: Create and manage text phrases that you can add to messages.

- **Spam filter**: Block messages by filtering based on criteria you set. Tap **Spam filter**, and then configure filters:

    - **Manage spam numbers**: Enter telephone numbers to automatically block.

    - **Manage spam phrases**: Enter text phrases to automatically block.

    - **Spam messages**: View blocked messages.

- **More settings > Text messages**:

    - **Auto combination**: Choose whether long messages that are received in multiple parts are automatically re-assembled to display as a single message.

- **More settings > Multimedia messages**:

    - **Group conversation**: Control how messages to multiple recipients are handled. When enabled, a single message is sent to multiple recipients. When disabled, a separate message is sent to each recipient.

    - **Auto retrieve**: Choose whether message attachment(s) are automatically downloaded when you display a multimedia message. If you disable this option, only the message header displays in the message list, and you will be prompted to download the attachment(s).

- **More settings > Delete old messages**: Automatically delete the oldest messages when the maximum number of text (1000) and multimedia (100) messages has been exceeded.

- **Emergency alert settings**: Configure emergency alert settings. You can enable or disable some alerts: Extreme Alert, Severe Alert, Amber Alert, and Emergency alert test messages. You cannot disable Presidential alerts.

    - **Emergency alerts**: Choose types of messages to receive. You can enable or display any of the message types, except for Presidential Alert. You can also choose to receive emergency alert test messages.

Important: The Commercial Mobile Alert System (CMAS) system provides the government the ability to send geographically targeted notifications of emergencies, such as threats to public safety, severe weather events, a hazardous material spill or a missing child in the phone user's area.

    - **Emergency notification preview**: Play a sample emergency alert tone. Tap **Stop** to cancel the playback.

    - **Vibrations**: Select vibration options for emergency message notifications.

    - **Alert reminder**: Configure the reminder interval.

Gmail

Use Google's Gmail service and your Google Account to send, receive, and manage your Gmail messages. Before using Gmail, you must register a Google (Gmail) Account on your phone. See Google Account for details.

Gmail Cautions

Gmail is handled as email from a PC. Restricting email from PCs on your phone prevents your phone from receiving Gmail.

Create and Send a Gmail Message

Use your phone to create and send Gmail messages.

1. From home, tap **Apps** ⊞ > **Google** 🔵 > **Gmail** M.

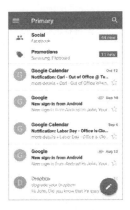

❖ The Gmail inbox opens.

2. In the inbox, tap Compose .

The Gmail composition window opens.

3. Enter the message recipient(s), subject, and message, and then tap Send ▶.

❖   The Gmail message is sent.

Gmail Composition Options

*   **Adding Cc/Bcc**: In the To field, tap ⋁ to display Cc and Bcc fields.

*   **Attaching Pictures or Videos**: In the mail composition window, tap **Attach file** 📎. Locate and tap the picture or video you want to attach.

- **Save as a draft (Send Later)**: While composing your message, tap **More options** ⁞ > **Save draft**. The message is saved as a draft for later.

- **Delete Mail Being Composed**: In the mail composition window, tap **More options** ⁞ > **Discard** > **Discard**.

Note: To view your draft email messages, in the inbox, tap **Menu** ☰ > **Drafts**.

Note: To view your sent messages, in the inbox, tap **Menu** ☰ > **Sent**.

Check Received Gmail Messages

Your phone allows you to access, read, and reply to all your Gmail messages.

Open New Gmail Messages from Notifications

When new Gmail arrives, you will see ☒ in the status bar.

1. Drag the status bar down to display the notification panel.

2. Tap the new message from the notification panel.

   ❖ The new Gmail message opens.

   ▪ If you have two or more new Gmail messages, tapping the notification opens the Gmail inbox.

Open Gmail Messages from the Inbox

You can also read and reply to all your Gmail messages from the Gmail inbox.

1. From home, tap **Apps** ⊞ > **Google** ⊞ > **Gmail** M.

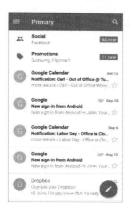

❖ The Gmail inbox opens.

2. Tap the message thread you want to view.

❖ The message thread opens, with the newest message displayed.

Options when Reviewing Gmail Messages

- **Replying to Gmail Messages**: With the Gmail message open, tap **Reply** ↖, compose your reply message, and tap **Send** ▶.

  - To reply to all, tap **More options** ⋮ > **Reply all**.

- **Forwarding Gmail Messages**: With the Gmail message open, tap **More options** ⋮ > **Forward**, enter a recipient and an additional message, and tap **Send** ▶.

Use Gmail Labels

Gmail saves all mail in one box, but you can add labels that allow you to sort your Gmail conversation threads. For example, when a new thread starts with a received mail, the label "Inbox" is automatically added to the thread. By then adding the label "travel," all threads with "travel" are shown in a list.

1. From home, tap **Apps** ⊞ > **Google** 🌐 > **Gmail** M.

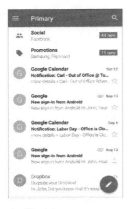

   ❖ The inbox opens.

2. Touch and hold a conversation thread (or touch the thread's icon/picture) to add a checkmark to it, and then tap **More options** ⋮ > **Move to**.

3. Tap a label for the thread.

❖ The thread is added to the selected label.

Tip: To add or manage your Gmail labels, open your Gmail account from your computer, click **More** at the bottom of the label list on the left, and then click **Manage labels** or **Create new labels**. Any changes you make from your computer will be reflected on your phone.

Archive Gmail Threads

Remove sent and received Gmail threads so they do not appear in the inbox. When replies arrive for archived threads, they appear in the inbox again.

1. From home, tap **Apps** ⊞ > **Google** 🟦 > **Gmail** M.

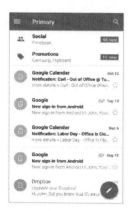

❖ The inbox opens.

2. Touch and hold a conversation thread (or touch the thread's icon/picture) to add a checkmark to it, and then tap **Archive** 🔲.

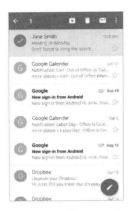

❖ The thread is now archived.

Mute Gmail Threads

If registered on a mailing list, there will be threads with always-continuing conversations. For long threads that are not important, mute the threads and they will no longer appear in the inbox. When mail arrives that includes user's address as a recipient or in Cc, mail will again appear in the inbox.

1. From home, tap **Apps** 🔘 > **Google** 🔘 > **Gmail** 📧.

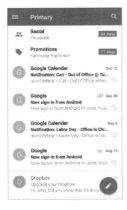

❖ The inbox opens.

2. Touch and hold a conversation thread (or touch the thread's icon/picture) to add a checkmark to it, and then tap **More options** 🔡 > **Mute**.

❖ The thread is now hidden.

Delete Gmail Threads

If you no longer wish to keep a Gmail conversation thread (or touch the thread's icon/picture), you can simply delete it from the inbox.

1. From home, tap **Apps** 🔘 > **Google** 🔘 > **Gmail** ✉.

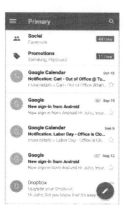

❖ The inbox opens.

2. Touch and hold a conversation thread (or touch the thread's icon/picture) to add a checkmark to it, and then tap **Delete** 🗑.

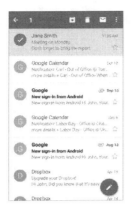

❖ The thread is deleted.

Note: Depending on your settings, you may be asked to confirm the deletion. Tap **Delete** to confirm. See Gmail Settings.

Search Gmail Messages

If you need to find a specific message or message thread, you can search Gmail from the inbox.

1. From home, tap **Apps** ⊞ > **Google** ● > **Gmail** M.

❖ The inbox opens.

2. Tap **Search** .

3. Enter your search text and tap **Search** .

❖ The search results appear. Tap a message or thread from the list to display it.

Report Spam Gmail

You can report spam Gmail messages from your phone's Gmail inbox.

1. From home, tap **Apps** ⊞ > **Google** 🔵 > **Gmail** ◤.

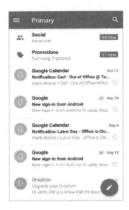

   ❖ The inbox opens.

2. Touch and hold a conversation thread (or touch the thread's icon/picture) to add a checkmark to it, and then tap **More options** ⋮ > **Report spam**.

   ❖ The selected message is reported as spam.

Add Another Google (Gmail) Account

If you have multiple Gmail accounts you wish to view on your phone, you can add them from the **Settings** > **Accounts** menu.

1. From home, tap **Apps**  > **Settings** > **Accounts** > **Add account**.

2. Tap **Google**.

3. Enter your Gmail username and password, and then tap **Next**.

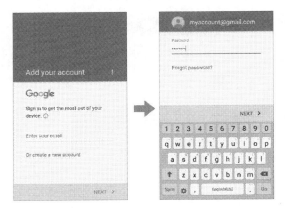

4. Follow the prompts to review and agree to the Terms of Service and Privacy Policy, and then tap **Accept**.

5. After your phone connects with the Google servers, select the items you would like to sync with your phone and then tap **Next**.

   ❖ You are signed in to your Google Account, and you can access both of your Gmail accounts from the Gmail app.

Tip: You can also add accounts from the Gmail app. From the Gmail inbox, tap **Menu** ▤ > **Settings** ⚙ > **Add account**.

Switching Between Gmail Accounts

If you have more than one Gmail account set up, you can switch between them in the Gmail app.

1. From home, tap **Apps** > **Google** > **Gmail** .

   ❖ The Primary inbox opens.

2. Tap **Menu** .

3. Tap the icon for the account you want to view from the list at the top of the menu.

   ❖ The selected account's Primary inbox is displayed.

Gmail Settings

You can access settings for the Gmail app and for your individual Gmail accounts from the Gmail Settings menu.

1. From home, tap **Apps** ⊞ > **Google** ⊛ > **Gmail** [M].

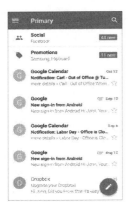

   ❖ The Primary inbox opens.

2. Tap **Menu** ☰ > **Settings** ⚙.

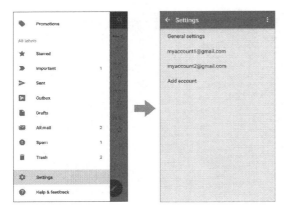

3. Tap **General settings** to access settings for all accounts, or tap an account name to configure settings for a specific Gmail account.

- **General settings**: Gmail default action, Conversation view, Swipe actions, Sender image, Reply all, Auto-fit messages, Auto-advance, Confirm before deleting, Confirm before archiving, and Confirm before sending.

- **Account settings**: Inbox type, Inbox categories, Notifications, Inbox sound & vibrate, Signature, Vacation responder, Sync Gmail, Days of mail to sync, Manage labels, Download attachments, and Images.

Note: Available settings are subject to change.

Email

Use the Email application to send and receive email from your webmail or other accounts, using POP3 or IMAP, or access your Exchange ActiveSync account for your corporate email needs.

Set Up an Email Account

Your phone supports several types of email accounts and allows you to have multiple email accounts set up at one time.

Before setting up an email account, make sure you have the username (user ID), password, server name, and more, so you can get set up successfully.

1. From home, tap **Apps** > **Email** .

❖ A window for adding an account appears if no email account has been previously set up.

2. Follow the prompts to set up your email account.

❖ The email account is set up and you will begin receiving email.

Add an Email Account

You can add several types of personal email accounts, such as POP3 and IMAP accounts, on your phone.

Add an Email Account from the Email App

You can add email accounts directly from the email app, even if you have another email account set up.

1. From home, tap **Apps** ⊞ > **Email** .

   ❖ The email inbox opens.

2. Tap **More** > **Settings** > **Add account**.

3. Follow the prompts to complete the account setup.

Messaging and Internet   133

❖ The email account is added and you will begin receiving email for the account.

Add an Email Account from the Settings Menu

You can also set up email accounts from the **Settings** > **Accounts** menu.

1. From home, tap **Apps** ⊞ > **Settings** ⚙ > **Accounts**.

2. Tap ➕ **Add account** > **Email**.

3. Enter the **Email address** and **Password** for the email account and then tap **Next**.

❖ Tapping **Next** prompts your phone to attempt a "regular" email setup and test the incoming and outgoing servers.

• If you have custom settings you need to configure, tap **Manual setup** and enter your settings. These may include mail type, user name, password, server, security type, and more.

4. Select your sync settings and then tap **Next**.

5. Enter an account name and a display name and tap **Done** to complete setup.

❖ The email account is set up and you will begin receiving email for the account.

Important: If the account type you want to set up is not in the phone database, you will be asked to enter more details. You should get all pertinent information for the email account, such as incoming and outgoing server settings, before you proceed.

Add an Exchange ActiveSync Account

If you synchronize your phone with your Exchange ActiveSync account, you can read, manage, and send email in the same easy way as with a POP3/IMAP account. However, you can also access some powerful Exchange features.

Important: Before setting up a Microsoft Exchange ActiveSync Account, contact your company's Exchange Server administrator for required account settings information.

1. From home, tap **Apps** ⊞ > **Settings** ⚙ > **Accounts** > **Add account** > **Microsoft Exchange ActiveSync**.

2. Enter the **Email address** and **Password** for the email account and then tap **Manual setup**.

3. Enter the required information.

   - **Email address**: Enter your email address.

   - **Domain\username**: Enter your network domain and username, separated by "\".

   - **Password**: Enter your network access password (case-sensitive).

   - **Show password**: Display the password as you enter it.

   - **Exchange server**: Enter your system's Exchange server remote email address. Obtain this information from your company network administrator.

- **Use secure connection (SSL)**: Tap to place a checkmark in the box, if your system requires SSL encryption.

- **Use client certificate**: Tap to place a checkmark in the box, if your system requires certification.

4. Tap **Next** and follow the prompts to configure options for the account.

5. Enter an account name and a display name and tap **Done** to complete setup.

  ❖ Your corporate email account is set up and you will begin receiving email for the account.

Compose and Send Email

Compose and send email using any account you have set up on your phone. Increase your productivity by attaching files such as pictures, videos, or documents to your email messages.

1. From home, tap **Apps**  > **Email** .

   ❖ The email inbox opens.

   ▪ If you want to switch to a different email account, tap the account name at the top of the screen and select another account.

   ▪ You can also view multiple inboxes at once. Tap the account name at the top of the screen and then tap **Combined inbox** to see messages from all your configured email accounts.

2. Tap **Compose** .

   ❖ The email composition window opens.

3. Enter the message recipient(s), subject, and message.

- To attach pictures or other files to the email, tap **Attach**, select a file type, and then tap a file to attach it.

- For additional options when composing email messages, tap **More** and select an option.

4. Tap **Send**.

❖ The email message is sent.

Open Email Messages

Open and view your email messages.

Open New Email Messages from Notifications

When new email arrives, you will see  in the status bar.

1. Drag the status bar down to display the notification panel.

2. Tap the new message from the notification panel.

    ❖ The new email message opens.

    ▪ If you have two or more new email messages, tapping the notification opens the email inbox. Tap a message to open it.

Open Email Messages from the Inbox

You can also open and read email messages directly from the email inbox. Reading and replying to email on your phone is as simple as on your computer.

1. From home, tap **Apps** 🎛 > **Email** 📧.

❖ The email inbox opens.

2. Tap the message you want to view.

❖ The email message opens.

Tip: Tap the account name at the top of the screen to switch to a different email account.

3. Tap **Reply** or **Reply all** to reply to the message.

Options When Reviewing Email Messages

- **Resetting Mail as Unread**: Touch and hold a read message, and then tap **More** > **Mark as unread**.

- **Deleting Email**: From the Inbox, touch and hold a message, select any additional messages, and then tap **Delete** > **Delete**.

  - When reading an email, tap **Delete** > **Delete**.

- **Replying to Email Messages**: With an email message open, tap **Reply** or **Reply all** , compose your reply message, and tap **Send.**

- **Forwarding Email Messages**: With the email message open, tap **Forward** , enter a recipient and an additional message, and tap **Send**.

Delete an Email Account

You can delete an email account from your phone if you no longer wish to receive messages for the account on your phone.

1. From home, tap **Apps**  > **Email** .

❖ The email inbox opens.

2. Tap **More** > **Settings**.

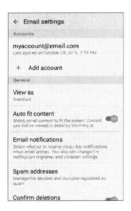

3. Tap the account name, and then tap **Remove** > **Remove**.

   ❖ The account is deleted from your phone

Manage Your Email Inbox

Your email inbox provides management options for viewing, sorting, and deleting your email messages.

View Your Email Inbox

1. From home, tap **Apps** ⊞ > **Email** 📧.

   ❖ The email inbox opens.

2. Tap the email account at the top of the screen to select a different inbox, or tap **Combined view** to see all your email inboxes at once.

Sort Email Messages

1. On the email account inbox, tap **More** > **Sort by**.

2. Select options for sorting email messages.

Delete Email Messages

1. On the email account inbox, touch and hold the message you want to delete.

   - Tap additional emails to delete.

2. Tap **Delete**.

Note: Depending on your settings, you may be prompted to confirm the deletion by tapping **Delete**. See Email Settings.

Exchange ActiveSync Email Features

Set options for your corporate Exchange ActiveSync email messages, including synchronization options, out-of-office messages, account settings, and more.

To access Exchange ActiveSync settings:

1. From home, tap **Apps** ⊞ > **Email** .

2. Tap **More** > **Settings**.

3. Tap the Exchange ActiveSync account name to view its options.

- The following options are available:

  - **Sync account**: Keep the account synchronized on your phone.

  - **Account name**: Change the account name.

  - **Always Cc/Bcc myself**: Send a copy of each email you send to yourself.

  - **Signature**: Enable and configure your signature for each email you send.

  - **Show images**: Show all images in emails.

  - **Sync schedule**: Configure a schedule for syncing your email account.

- **Period to sync Email**: Configure how far back in time you want to sync your email account.

- **Limit retrieval size**: Set a limit to the size of email messages you want to receive on your phone.

- **Limit retrieval size while roaming**: Set a different email size limit when your phone is on roaming.

- **Out of office settings**: You can set your Out of Office status and auto-reply message right from your phone.

- **Folder sync settings**: Select which email folders to sync with the server.

- **Period to sync Calendar**: Set the time period for syncing your calendar with the server.

- **Empty server trash**: Delete the content of the trash folder on the server.

- **In case of sync conflict**: Select whether the device or the server has priority during a sync conflict.

- **Sync Contacts**: Sync your Contacts with your Exchange account.

- **Sync Calendar**: Sync your calendar with your Exchange account.

- **Sync Task**: Sync your tasks with your Exchange account.

- **Sync Messages**: Sync your messages with your Exchange account.

- **Security options**: Manage encryption and signature options for outgoing email.

- **Exchange server settings**: Modify the Exchange server settings for this email account.

Email Settings

Configure options for email accounts you set up on your phone.

General Email Preferences

1. From home, tap **Apps** ⊞ > **Email** 📧.

❖ The email inbox opens.

2. Tap **More** > **Settings** to configure options. General email settings, which affect all email accounts, include:

- **Manage accounts**: Configure options for specific accounts. Available settings depend on the type of account.

- **Add account**: Add additional email accounts.

- **View as**: View emails in Standard format, or as Conversations.

- **Auto fit content**: Shrink email content to fit the screen. Content can still be viewed in detail by zooming in.

- **Email notifications**: Notifications for new emails display in the status bar. When disabled, you can control notifications for each of your email accounts individually in the account's settings.

- **Spam addresses**: Create and maintain a list of email addresses and domains to automatically block emails from those senders.

- **Confirm deletions**: Ask for confirmation before deleting email.

Manage Email Account Settings

You can edit settings for your individual email accounts, such as email address and password, name display and signature, frequency of retrieval, and more.

Note: Available settings depend on the type of email account.

1. From home, tap **Apps** ⊞ > **Email** ⬚ > **More** > **Settings**.

2. Tap an account to set its options. Individual email account settings may vary; see your service provider for details. Common settings include:

- **Sync account**: Configure options for synchronizing your phone with your account.

- **Account name**: Enter a name to identify this email account.

- **Always Cc/Bcc myself**: Choose options for sending a copy of emails you send to yourself, as a copy (Cc) or blind copy (Bcc).

- **Signature**: A text signature is automatically added to emails you send.

- **Show images**: Choose whether to automatically display embedded images in the body of an email.

- **Sync schedule**: Set a sync schedule for email, such as choosing different sync options for peak days or times, or when roaming.

- **Period to sync Email**: Choose the period for synchronizing email between your phone and account.

- **Limit retrieval size**: Choose the email retrieval size for each message.

- **Limit retrieval size while roaming**: Choose the email retrieval size while roaming.

- **Out of office settings**: Configure options for automatically sending replies when you are out of the office.

- **Folder sync settings**: Choose which folders to sync.

- **Period to sync Calendar**: Choose the period for synchronizing calendar events between your phone and account.

- **Empty server trash**: Delete the contents of the trash folder on the account server.

- **In case of sync conflict**: Choose whether information from the server or phone has priority when there is a conflict.

- **Sync Contacts**: Choose whether contacts are synchronized between your phone and the account.

- **Sync Calendar**: Choose whether calendar events are synchronized between your phone and the account.

- **Sync Task**: Choose whether tasks are synchronized between your phone and the account.

- **Sync Messages**: Choose whether messages are synchronized between your phone and the account.

- **Security options**: Manage encryption and signature options for outgoing mail.

- **Exchange server settings**: Configure the Domain\user name, Password, and other Exchange server settings.

Browser

Your phone's Web browser gives you full access to both mobile and traditional websites on the go using 3G, 4G, or Wi-Fi data connections.

SSL/TLS

SSL (Secure Sockets Layer) and TLS (Transport Layer Security) are protocols for encrypting sent/received data. While in a screen connected by SSL/TLS, data is encrypted to safely send/receive private information, credit card numbers, corporate secrets, and more, and provide protection against online threats (eavesdropping, falsification, impersonation, and more).

▓ SSL/TLS Cautions

When opening a secured page, users must decide as their responsibility whether or not to open the page with use of SSL/TLS. Boost and the applicable Certification Authorities make no guarantees whatsoever to users regarding security of SSL/TLS.

Use the Browser

Launching the browser is as easy as tapping an icon.

- From home, tap **Apps** ⊞ > **Internet** 🌐.

❖ The browser opens.

- The first time you launch Internet, you may be prompted to enter your 10-digit wireless phone number to access the Boost home page.

- You can also launch the browser by tapping a URL in a text message, email message, or Gmail message.

Tip: To change the phone's default launch page to your current page, tap **More** > **Settings** > **Homepage** > **Current page**.

Add a Bookmark

Bookmark favorite sites using the browser menu options.

1. From home, tap **Apps** ⊞ > **Internet** ⊛.

   ❖ The browser opens.

2. Navigate to the Web page you want to bookmark, and tap **Bookmarks** 🔖 > **Add.**

   ❖ The add bookmark window opens.

3. Check or change the bookmark title, URL, and more, and then tap **Save**.

   ❖ The Web page is added to bookmarks.

Bookmark Options

- **Editing Bookmarks**: From the browser, tap **Bookmarks** 🔖, touch and hold a bookmark, tap **More** > **Edit bookmark**, edit the bookmark, and then tap **Save**.

- **Deleting Bookmarks**: From the browser, tap **Bookmarks** 🔖, touch and hold a bookmark, and then tap **Delete**.

View Browser History

Use the browser menu options to view your browsing history.

1. From home, tap **Apps** ⊞ > **Internet** 🌐.

❖ The browser opens.

2. Tap **Bookmarks** 🔖.

❖ The bookmark window opens.

3. Tap the **History** tab, and then tap an entry.

❖ The Web page opens.

Open New Browser Tab

Use tabs to switch between websites quickly and easily.

1. From home, tap **Apps** ⊞ > **Internet** 🔵.

   ❖ The browser opens.

2. Tap **Tabs** 🔲.

   ❖ The window opens.

   ▪ If you do not see **Tabs** 🔲, drag the Web page down to display the address bar on top and the options bar on the bottom.

3. Tap **New tab**.

   ❖ A new window appears.

- To switch windows, tap **Tabs** , and then touch a thumbnail.

Browser Settings

Configure Internet settings, to customize the browser to your preferences.

1. From home, tap **Apps** ⊞ > **Internet** ⑤.

❖ The browser opens.

2. Tap **More** > **Settings** to configure options:

- **Homepage**: Choose a homepage to display when you launch Internet.

- **Default search engine**: Choose a default search engine.

- **Auto fill profile**: Manage your Auto fill profile.

- **Manual zoom**: Override website requests to control zoom level

- **Privacy**: Choose options related to privacy.

- **Advanced**: Choose settings to control how the browser treats content, such as allowing JavaScript, blocking pop-ups, and managing website data.

Chrome Browser

In addition to the default "Internet" Web browser, your phone supports the Chrome mobile Web browser. If you are signed in with a Google Account, the Chrome browser will import all your bookmarks and other Web preferences for use on your phone.

1. From home, tap **Apps** ▦ > **Chrome** ◎.

2. The first time you open Chrome, you will be prompted to agree to Chrome's Terms of Service and Privacy Notice. Read the terms and tap **Agree & Continue** to continue.

3. If you want to sign in with a Google Account to import bookmarks and other preferences, select an account and tap **Sign in**. If you do not want to sign in with a Google Account, tap **No Thanks**.

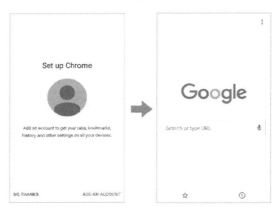

   ❖ Chrome opens.

4. Tap the address bar at the top and enter search words (for a Google search) or a Web address (URL).

❖ The search results appear or a Web page opens.

Chrome Support

■ To find on-phone help with Chrome, from Chrome, tap **More options** ⋮ > **Help & feedback**.

❖ A Web page will open displaying Google help for Chrome.

Tip: For more information, from your computer, visit: google.com/chrome.

Camera and Video

You can use the camera or video camera to take and share pictures and videos. Your phone comes with a 5 megapixel rear camera and a 2 megapixel front camera that let you capture sharp pictures and videos.

Note: Prior to using the camera, remove the plastic protective covering from the camera lens.

Camera Overview

The camera's viewfinder screen lets you view your subject and access camera controls and options.

- **Shortcuts menu**: Gives quick access to frequently-used camera settings:

    - **Effect**: Add a special graphical effect.

    - **Timer**: Take time-delayed pictures or videos.

    - **Flash**: Activate or deactivate the flash. Toggle through flash options—on, auto, or off (rear camera only).

- **Camera settings**: Opens the camera settings menu and lets you change additional camera settings. See Camera Options and Settings.

- **Gallery**: View your picture or video in the Gallery application.

- **Record video**: Begin recording video.

- **Capture picture**: Take a picture.

- **Switch cameras:** Switch between the rear camera and the front camera.

- **Shooting modes**: Select a shooting mode.

Take Pictures and Record Videos

The following topics teach you how to take pictures and record videos with your phone's camera.

Capturing Pictures/Videos

- **File Format for Pictures**: File format for pictures is JPEG (.jpg).

- **File Format for Videos**: File format for videos is MPEG4 (.mp4).

Camera Cautions

If Lens Becomes Dirty: Fingerprints/smudges on lens prevent capturing of clear still images/videos. Wipe lens with a soft cloth beforehand.

Avoid Exposure to Direct Sunlight: Be careful not to expose lens to direct sunlight for long periods. This may discolor color filter and affect color of images.

Flash Warning

Do not shine the flash close to eyes. Do not look directly at the flash when shining. Do not shine the flash at other people's eyes. It may affect eyesight.

Take a Picture

You can take high-resolution pictures using your phone's camera.

Note: Prior to using the camera, remove the plastic protective covering from the camera lens.

1. From home, tap **Apps** ⊞ > **Camera** .

   ❖ The camera viewfinder appears.

2. Aim the camera at your subject and then tap .

❖ The shutter clicks and the picture is captured and saved to your phone.

Tip: You can launch the camera from the lock screen. Swipe 📷 up from the lock screen to open the camera.

Record Videos

Record high-quality videos using your phone's video camera.

1. From home, tap **Apps** ⊞ > **Camera** 📷.

❖ The camera viewfinder appears.

2. Aim the camera at your subject and then tap **Record** ⏺.

❖ Video recording begins.

▪ Tap  to pause recording. Tap ● to resume a paused recording.

3. Tap ● to stop recording.

❖ The camera stops recording and the video is captured and saved to your phone.

Shooting Modes

Your phone's camera offers many shooting modes, to make your pictures or videos special.

1. From home, tap **Apps** ⊞ > **Camera** 📷.

❖ The camera viewfinder appears.

2. On the Camera screen, tap 🔘 to choose a shooting mode. Scroll available modes, and then tap a mode to select it.

- **Rear camera**

    - **Auto**: Automatically adjusts the exposure to optimize the color and brightness of pictures.

    - **Pro**: Adjust the ISO sensitivity, exposure value, white balance, focal length, and color tone manually while taking pictures.

    - **Panorama**: Take multiple pictures to merge into one expansive picture. You can create a horizontal or vertical panorama picture.

    - **Continuous shot**: Touch and hold the capture button to take continuous photos.

    - **Beauty face**: Automatically enhances facial features.

    - **Sound & shot**: Adds a few seconds of background sound to enhance pictures.

    - **Sports**: Allows you to capture clear shots of a moving subject.

- **Front camera**

    - **Selfie**: Take selfie shots and apply various effects, such as an airbrushed effect.

    - **Sound & shot**: Adds a few seconds of background sound to enhance pictures.

Note: All modes may not be shown when you tap 🔘, depending on your phone's setup and which camera is active (front or rear).

View Pictures and Videos Using Gallery

Using the Gallery application, you can view pictures and watch videos that you have taken with your phone's camera, downloaded, or copied to phone memory. You can also take a look at your pictures and your friends' pictures that are on your social networks.

For pictures that are on your phone, you can do basic editing such as rotating and cropping. You can also easily assign a picture as your contact picture or wallpaper and share pictures with your friends.

1. From home, tap **Apps** ⬛ > **Gallery** ⬤.

❖ The Gallery opens.

2. Tap **Time** to open a drop-down list and select other views, such as **Albums**.

❖ The list of albums opens.

3. Tap an album to view its contents.

▪ To select another album, tap the **Back** key ⬐ to return to the Albums.

4. For a picture, tap a thumbnail to view the picture. While viewing a picture full-screen you can use the following options:

- **Share**: Choose a method for sharing the picture.
- **Edit**: Modify your picture.
- **Delete**: Erase the current picture.
- **Camera**: Tap to open the camera app.
- **More**: Choose other options, including:
  - **Details**: View file details.
  - **Slideshow**: Create a slideshow.
  - **Set as contact picture**: Set the picture as the photo for a contact.
  - **Set as wallpaper**: Set the picture as wallpaper for your home or lock screens.

5. For a video, tap a video to select it. When the video is displayed full-screen, you can use the following options:

- Tap **Play** ⊙ to play the video.

- **Share**: Choose a method for sharing the video.

- **Editor**: Edit the video.

- **Delete**: Erase the current video.

- **More**: Choose other options, including:

    - **Details**: View file details.

    - **Slideshow**: Create a slideshow.

Pictures and Videos: Review Screen

After capturing a picture or video, from the camera screen, tap the thumbnail to see the item in the review screen. From there, you can access options such as save, view, send, or delete the picture or video.

Pictures and Videos: Options while Viewing

- **Zoom In or Out on a Picture**: Tap the screen twice or pinch the screen to zoom in or out on a picture.

- **Viewing Videos**: Use the controls to play, pause, or stop the video playback.

After selecting an album from the Albums tab, you can browse through the pictures and videos of that album. Tap a picture or video to view it in full screen.

Note: When viewing pictures, you can tap a picture or video to open a selection menu and choose what to do with the picture or video.

Edit Pictures

Whether you are browsing pictures in filmstrip or grid view in the Gallery application, you can tap a picture to open a selection menu and choose to delete the picture, rotate or crop it, and more.

Rotate a Picture

The editing options let you rotate pictures 90 degrees clockwise. Repeat the action for additional rotations.

1. From home, tap **Apps** ⊞ > **Gallery** 🖼.

   ❖ The Gallery app opens.

2. Tap the picture you want to rotate.

3. Tap **Edit** 🔴 > **Rotate**.

❖ The picture is rotated and saved to the phone.

Crop a Picture

Use the editing tools to crop your pictures.

1. From home, tap **Apps** ⊞ > **Gallery** 🔵.

❖ The Gallery app opens.

2. Tap the picture you want to crop.

3. Tap **Edit**  > **Crop**.

❖ A crop box appears on the picture.

4. To adjust the crop box size, touch and hold the edge of the box. When directional arrows appear, drag your finger inward to or outward to resize the crop box.

▪ To move the crop box to the part of the picture that you want to crop, drag the crop box to the desired size and position.

5. Tap **Save** to apply the changes to the picture.

❖ The cropped picture is saved in the album as a copy. The original picture remains unedited.

Photo Editor

Perform advanced edits on your pictures, including straightening, adjusting the tone, adding visual effects, and enhancing portraits.

1. From home, tap **Apps** ⊞ > **Gallery** .

 ❖ The Gallery app opens.

2. Tap the picture you want to edit.

3. Tap **Edit** 🖊 > **Photo Editor**.

 ❖ Enhancement tools display.

4. Adjust your picture with these tools:

- **Adjustment**: Straighten and freely rotate your picture.

- **Tone**: Adjust the brightness, contrast, saturation, temperature, and hue of the picture.

- **Effect**: Add color effects to your picture.

- **Portrait**: Apply effects such as brightening, softening, and fixing red eye when a face or faces are detected in a picture. (This option appears if a person's face is detected in the picture.)

- **Drawing**: Draw or write on your picture.

Collage

Create a photo collage with your pictures.

1. From home, tap **Apps** 🔢 > **Gallery** ⚫.

   ❖ The Gallery app opens.

2. Tap a picture you want to add to a collage.

3. Tap **Edit** ✎ > **Collage**.

4. Tap ➕ or **Add** to select additional pictures for the collage.

   ▪ Tap pictures to select them.

   ▪ Tap **Done** when you are finished selecting.

❖ Your collage layout will be displayed.

5. Use the tools at the bottom of the screen to adjust your collage.

- **Aspect ratio**: Adjust the aspect ratio of the collage.

- **Layout**: Change the layout of the collage.

- **Border**: Choose the border roundness and margin for the collage.

- **Background**: Change the background of the collage.

6. To adjust an individual picture within the collage, tap a picture and use the pop-up menu options:

- **Replace**: Replace the selected picture.

- **Remove**: Remove the selected picture from the collage.

- **Effect**: Assign an effect to the picture.

- **Adjustment**: Crop, rotate, flip, reverse, or resize the picture.

  • With a picture selected, you can also drag it to reposition it within its place in the collage.

7. Tap **Save** to save the collage to the Photo editor album.

Share Pictures and Videos

The Gallery application lets you send pictures and videos using email or multimedia messages. You can share pictures on your social networks (such as Facebook and Google+) and share videos on YouTube. You can also send them to another phone or your computer using Bluetooth.

Send Pictures or Videos by Email or Gmail

You can send several pictures, videos, or both in an email or Gmail message. They are added as file attachments in your email. For more information about using email and Gmail, see Compose and Send Email or Create and Send a Gmail Message.

1. From home, tap **Apps** 🔳 > **Gallery** .

❖ The Gallery app opens.

2. Tap the pictures or videos you want to share.

▪ To select multiple items, touch and hold an image to turn on multiple select. Tap all the items you want to include.

3. Tap **Share**, and then on the sharing menu, tap **Email** or **Gmail**.

❖ Follow prompts to complete and send the message.

Note: If you have multiple email accounts or Gmail accounts, the default account will be used. Check the "From" line to determine which account is being used.

For more information about using email and Gmail, see Compose and Send Email or Create and Send a Gmail Message.

Send a Picture or Video by Multimedia Message

Multimedia Messaging (MMS) lets you send pictures and videos using your phone's messaging app. Although you can send several pictures or videos in a multimedia message, it may be better to just send one at a time, especially if the files are large in size.

1. From home, tap **Apps** > **Gallery**.

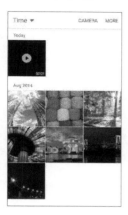

   ❖ The Gallery app opens.

2. Tap the pictures or videos you want to share.

   ▪ To select multiple items, touch and hold an image to turn on multiple select. Tap all the items you want to include.

3. Tap **Share**, and then on the sharing menu, tap **Messages**.

   ❖ Follow the prompts to complete and send the message.

For more information about sending multimedia messages, see Send a Multimedia Message (MMS).

Send Pictures or Videos Using Bluetooth

You can select several pictures, videos, or both and send them to someone's phone or your computer using Bluetooth.

1. From home, tap **Apps** ⊞ > **Gallery** 📷.

   ❖ The Gallery app opens.

2. Tap the pictures or videos you want to share.

   ▪ To select multiple items, touch and hold an image to turn on multiple select. Tap all the items you want to include.

3. Tap **Share**, and then on the sharing menu, tap **Bluetooth**.

❖ Follow the prompts to complete and send the files.

For more information, see Bluetooth.

Share Videos on YouTube

You can share your videos by uploading them to YouTube. Before you do this, you must create a YouTube account and sign in to that account on your phone.

1. From home, tap **Apps** ⊞ > **Gallery** 🔵.

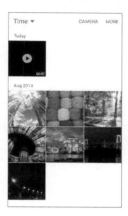

❖ The Gallery app opens.

2. Tap the videos you want to share.

▪ To select multiple videos, touch and hold an image to turn on multiple select. Tap all the videos you want to include.

3. Tap **Share**, and then on the sharing menu, tap **YouTube**.

4. Enter the prompted information, such as description and tags, and select a privacy option.

5. Tap **Upload** ![upload icon].

   ❖ The upload is completed.

Camera Options and Settings

You can adjust your camera's settings using the icons on the main camera screen and the full camera settings menu.

Switch Cameras

Your phone lets you switch between the front and rear cameras.

1. From home, tap **Apps** ▦ > **Camera** ⬤.

   ❖ The camera viewfinder appears.

2. Tap ●.

   ❖ The camera switches type.

Set Camera Options

You can configure your camera's settings to fit any situation and event.

1. From home, tap **Apps** ⊞ > **Camera** ●.

   ❖ The camera viewfinder appears.

2. Tap **Settings** ⚙. If you do not see the Settings option, tap ∨ to display the options icons.

   ❖ The camera settings menu opens.

3. Select your desired settings:

Note: Not all settings will be available at all times, depending on which camera is in use (front or rear).

   ▪ **Both cameras**

- **Picture size**: Change the resolution of pictures. Different settings are available for the front and rear cameras.

- **Video size**: Select a resolution. Use higher resolution for higher quality. Higher resolution videos take up more memory.

- **Grid lines**: Display viewfinder grid lines to help composition when selecting subjects.

- **Location tags**: Attach a GPS location tag to the picture.

- **Review pictures**: Set to show pictures after taking them.

- **Quick launch**: Open camera by pressing the Home key twice in quick succession.

- **Storage location**: Specify where to store photos and videos, if other options are available.

- **Volume keys function**: Use the Volume key as the capture key, the record key, or as a zoom key.

- **Reset settings**: Reset the camera settings.

- **Front camera only**

  - **Gesture control**: Detect palm and automatically take a picture two seconds later.

  - **Save pictures as previewed**: Save the self-portrait or self-recording as viewed on the camera screen.

Apps and Features

The following topics detail many of your phone's tools and features such as maps and navigation, calendar, clock, social networking apps, music, memos, and more.

1Weather

Check weather and forecasts with 1Weather: Widget Forecast Radar, which combines a groundbreaking UI with a power set of weather tools.

- From home, tap **Apps** ⊞ > **1Weather** 🌐.

airG

Meet new friends instantly with just one click. Real-time feeds allow you to browse through the latest community activity or just see what your friends are up to.

- From home, tap **Apps** ⊞ > **airG** 🖼️.

Boost 411

Boost 411 gives you access to a variety of services and information, including residential, business, and government listings; movie listings or show times; driving directions, restaurant reservations, and major local event information. You can get up to three pieces of information per call, and the operator can automatically connect your call at no additional charge.

- From home, tap **Apps** ⊞ > **Boost 411** 🖼️.

Boost Music

Discover millions of DRM-free music tracks, ringtones, and ringback tones from Boost's official music store and player.

- From home, tap **Apps** ⊞ > **Boost Music** 🖼️.

Boost Wallet

Boost Wallet is a quick and easy way to make payments with cash directly from your Boost Mobile phone. Send money, pay bills and top-up your mobile phone account balance.

- From home, tap **Apps** ⊞ > **Boost Wallet** 🖼️.

Boost Zone

Stay connected to all the latest news and information from Boost. Included here are news, feedback, featured applications and tips/tricks for your device.

- From home, tap **Apps** ⊞ > **Boost Zone** .

boostTV

Watch live and on demand entertainment from popular broadcast and cable networks, news channels and primetime TV shows.

Update boostTV

1. From home, tap **Apps** ⊞ > **boostTV** .

2. Tap **Update**, and then follow the prompts to accept access requirements and update the app.

Use boostTV

- From home, tap **Apps** ⊞ > **boostTV** .

Calculator

Your phone's convenient built-in calculator lets you perform basic mathematical equations.

1. From home, tap **Apps** ⊞ > **Calculator** .

❖ The Calculator app launches.

2. Tap keys for calculations.

❖ Calculation results appear.

Tip: To use the scientific calculator, make sure Auto rotate is turned on (drag the notification panel down and tap **Auto rotate**) and rotate the screen to the landscape orientation.

❖ Keys for the scientific calculator appear.

Calendar

Use Calendar to create and manage events, meetings, and appointments. Your Calendar helps organize your time and reminds you of important events. Depending on your synchronization settings, your phone's Calendar stays in sync with your Calendar on the Web, Exchange ActiveSync calendar, Google Calendar, and Outlook calendar.

In order to sync with your Google calendar, you must sign in to a Google Account on your phone. See Google Account.

Calendar Options

- **View Today's Calendar**: From the Calendar, tap **Today**.

- **Change Calendar View**: From the Calendar, tap the drop-down menu in the upper left corner, and then tap **Year**, **Month**, **Week**, **Day**, or **Tasks** to change the current view.

- **View the Next/Previous Time Period (Year/Month/Week/Day** view): From the Calendar, flick the screen left or right.

Add an Event to the Calendar

Add events to your calendar directly from the Calendar application.

1. From home, tap **Apps** ▦ > **Calendar** 🔟.

❖ The Calendar app opens.

2. Tap **New** .

❖ The add event window opens.

3. Enter an event title, start date/time, end date/time, and more, and then tap **Save**.

❖ The event is added to your Calendar.

Selecting a Calendar

■ If you have more than one calendar, select a calendar by tapping the current Calendar on the Add Event screen.

- Select **My calendars** to create an event that will appear only on your phone.

- Select your Google Account to create a Google Calendar event. If you have several Google Calendars on the Web, select one in which to add your event.

  - You can create multiple Google Calendars only in Google Calendar on the Web. After creating them in Google Calendar on the Web, you will be able to see them in the Calendar application on your phone. For more information about creating and managing multiple Google Calendars, visit calendar.google.com.

- Select **Samsung Calendar** to create an event that will sync with your Samsung account.

- Select your Outlook or Exchange account to create an event that will sync with these account types.

Note: Available options differ depending on the type of account selected for an event.

View Calendar Events

You can display the Calendar in year, month, week, day, or task view. To change the Calendar view, tap the drop-down menu at the upper-left corner and tap an option.

1. From home, tap **Apps**  > **Calendar** 🔟.

   The Calendar app opens.

2. Tap a date and then tap an event.

   ❖ The event details appear.

   ▪ Tap the event to view details and edit the event.

Share Calendar Events

Once you have created a Calendar event, you can share it with others using a variety of methods.

1. From home, tap **Apps** ▦ > **Calendar** 🔢.

2. Tap a date and then tap an event to see its details.

3. From the event details screen, tap **Share**.

4. Choose a **Share as** option (**Event file (VCS)** or **Text**).

5. Select a sharing method and follow the prompts to send the Event information.

Sync Calendars

You can select which calendars you would like to sync on your phone, along with what types of information you want to sync.

1. From home, tap **Apps** ⊞ > **Calendar** 🗓.

   ❖ The Calendar app opens.

2. Tap **More** > **Manage calendars**.

3. Select sync options by tapping **ON/OFF** next to each item.

❖ The sync settings have been updated.

Synchronize an Exchange ActiveSync Calendar

If you have set up a Microsoft Exchange ActiveSync account on your phone, you can also synchronize Exchange ActiveSync calendar events on your phone. Calendar events on your Exchange ActiveSync will also show in Calendar if you chose to synchronize with the Exchange ActiveSync Server.

1. To check if Exchange ActiveSync items are set to be synchronized, from home, tap **Apps** ⊞ > **Settings** ⚙ > **Accounts** ⊗ > **Microsoft Exchange ActiveSync**.

    ▪ If Microsoft Exchange ActiveSync does not appear under the Accounts heading in the Settings menu, you do not have an Exchange ActiveSync account configured on the phone. For information about adding an account, see Add an Exchange ActiveSync Account.

2. If your Exchange ActiveSync account is set for synchronization, the **ON/OFF** switch next to Sync Calendar will be **ON** .

Calendar Settings

Configure settings for your phone's Calendar app.

1. From home, tap **Apps**  > **Calendar** 🔟.

❖ The Calendar app opens.

2. Tap **More > Settings** to configure the following options:

- **First day of week**: Choose a day to start each calendar week.

- **Show week numbers**: Enable or disable display of week numbers on the calendar.

- **Hide declined events**: When enabled, events for which you declined the invitation are not shown on the calendar.

- **Notifications:**

- **Notification sound**: Choose a sound for calendar event notifications.

- **Vibration**: Enable or disable vibration, to play for calendar event notifications.

- **Set default reminders**: Set default reminders for Events and All-day events.

- **Lock time zone**: When enabled, event times will be locked to the time zone you select. Times and dates will not change, even if you travel to another time zone.

CallWatch

Receive alerts in real-time of suspicious and unwanted incoming calls and text messages.

Install CallWatch

1. From home, tap **Apps** ⊞ > **CallWatch** 📷.

2. Tap **Install**, and then follow the prompts to accept access requirements and update the app.

Use CallWatch

- From home, tap **Apps** ⊞ > **CallWatch** 📷.

Clock

Your phone has a clock app that lets you set alarms, view time in time zones around the world, use a stopwatch, set a timer, and use your phone as a desk clock.

Checking the Time

You can always check the time on your phone. The current time displays in the upper right corner of the status bar. Many widgets and lock screens also display the time and provide options for how time is displayed.

Setting Date and Time

Your phone automatically receives the current date and time from the wireless network. You can set the date by hand by overriding the default setting.

1. From home, tap **Apps** ⊞ > **Settings** ⚙.

2. Tap **Date and time** 🕓.

3. Set available date and time options.

- To set the date and time, tap **ON/OFF** to turn Automatic date and time off.

- To select a time zone, tap **ON/OFF** to turn Automatic time zone off.

- Your date and time settings are applied and saved.

Set Alarms

Set multiple alarms using your phone's Clock app.

1. From home, tap **Apps** ⊞ > **Clock** 🕐 > **Alarm**.

2. Tap **Add**.

3. Set the alarm options, including time, days, and repeat pattern.

4. When finished, tap **Save**.

   ❖ You will see the alarm icon ⏰ in the status bar.

Phone at Alarm Time

- At the set alarm time, the phone sounds the alarm and/or vibrates.

- When the alarm sounds, drag ⊗ to the left or right to dismiss it.

World Clock

The World clock lets you keep track of the current time in multiple cities around the globe.

1. From home, tap **Apps** ⊞ > **Clock** 🕑 > **World clock**.

2. Tap **Add** to add another city.

3. Swipe the list or tap the **Search** field to search for a city.

4. Tap a city to add it to the World clock list.

5. To remove a city, tap ⊠ **Remove** on the city's entry.

Stopwatch

The stopwatch lets you time events down to the hundredth of a second.

1. From home, tap **Apps** ⊞ > **Clock** 🕑 > **Stopwatch**.

2. Tap **Start** to begin timing.

3. Tap **Stop** to stop timing.

   - Additional options include **Lap** to keep track of laps, **Resume** to continue timing, and **Reset** to reset the stopwatch to zero.

Timer

The timer provides a countdown timer for up to 99 hours, 59 minutes, and 59 seconds.

1. From home, tap **Apps** ⊞ > **Clock** 🕒 > **Timer**.

2. Tap **Keypad** and then use the keypad to set the length of the timer.

3. Tap **Start** to begin the timer.

Facebook

Post updates, read what your friends are up to, upload pictures and check-ins, and more with on-the-go Facebook access.

Sign In to Facebook

1. From home, tap **Apps** ⊞ > **Facebook** 🔵.

   – or –

   From home, tap **Apps** ⊞ > **Settings** ⚙ > **Accounts** > **Add accounts** > **Facebook**.

2. If you have a Facebook account, enter your user ID and password, and then tap **Log in**.

– or –

To create a new Facebook account, tap **Sign Up for Facebook** > **Next**, and then follow the prompts.

❖ You are signed in to Facebook.

Gadget Guardian

Keep your device and personal data safe and secure.

■ From home, tap **Apps** ⊞ > **Gadget Guardian** 🛡.

Galaxy Apps

Discover apps designed exclusively for your Galaxy phone.

Note: You must sign in to a Samsung account in order to download Galaxy Apps.

■ From home, tap **Apps** ⊞ > **Galaxy Apps** 🛍.

Gallery

Using the Gallery application, you can view pictures and watch videos that you have taken with your phone's camera or downloaded.

You can do basic editing such as rotating and cropping. You can also set a picture as your contact picture or wallpaper and share pictures with your friends.

While viewing pictures in the Gallery, scroll up the screen to view more albums. Simply tap an album to view the photos or videos in that album.

If you have downloaded any photos and videos, these will be placed in the All downloads album.

1. From home, tap **Apps** ▦ > **Gallery** 🔘.

❖ The Gallery app opens.

2. From the main Gallery screen, you can use the following options:

- Tap a picture or video to display it in full screen view.

- Touch and hold thumbnails to select them (indicated by a checkmark).

- Tap the drop-down list in the upper-left corner (Time is the default view) to choose another display style. You can view by Albums, Events, Categories, or Locations.

- Tap **Camera** to launch the Camera to take pictures or record video.

- Tap **More** for options. Available options depend on which Gallery screen you are viewing, and may include:

  - **Edit**: Depending on the view, tap albums or items to select them. After selection, you can tap **More** again for options you can use with the selected item(s).

  - **Share**: Share albums, pictures, or videos.

For more information about using Gallery, see View Pictures and Videos Using Gallery, Edit Pictures, and Share Pictures and Videos.

Google Hangouts

Hangouts is Google's instant messaging service. Use to communicate with other Hangout users, as well as for video calling. Log in to a Google Account beforehand (see Google Account).

Using Hangouts

1. From home, tap **Apps** ⊞ > **Google** 🔲 > **Hangouts** 💬.

  ❖ The Hangouts app will open.

2. Tap **Add** ⊕ to start a new Hangout.

3. Type a name, email, number, or circle, or select a contact from the list.

4. Type a message or tap ◉ to start a video chat.

   ❖ A chat window or a video chat window opens.

   ▪ Each time text is entered, the corresponding friend appears.

   ▪ If a friend is not in a Hangout, you will see a message. Tap **Send invitation** to invite them to join the Hangout.

Hangouts Options

- **Ending a Video Chat**: In the video chat window, tap ◉.

- **Disabling Chat History**: If you do not want to keep chat history, in the chat window, tap **More options** ⋮ > **Turn history off**.

- **Delete Chat History**: To delete all your chat history, in the chat window, tap **More options** ⋮ > **Delete** > **Delete**.

Note: You can use Hangouts as your phone's default messaging app, or as a standalone IM app. If you set Hangouts as the default messaging app, the Messages app will be disabled. For more information, see Default Messaging App Settings.

Google Maps

Use the Google Maps app to determine your location, find directions, browse local businesses and attractions, rate and review places, and more.

Note: To use Google Maps, you will need to have your phone's Location feature turned on. See Location Settings for information about enabling Location on your phone.

View Maps of Specified Places

Use Google Maps to locate and map a specific address or destination.

1. From home, tap **Apps** ⊞ > **Maps** 🗺.

❖ Google Maps opens.

Note: The first time you access Maps, you may be prompted to accept the Terms of Service and Privacy Policy. Tap **Accept & Continue** to continue.

2. Tap in the search box to start a search.

3. Enter an address, city, facility name, and more, and then tap a candidate in the results list.

❖   A map of the specified location opens.

Google Maps Options

- **Viewing Current Location**: From the Maps app, tap ⊙.

- **Obtain Useful Area Information for Current Location**: Tap the **Search** field, enter the information you are looking for, and then tap a result to view it.

- **View Traffic Information, Aerial Photos, and more**: Tap **Menu** ≡ and then tap **Traffic**, **Satellite**, **Google Earth**, and more.

- **Check Route to Destination**: Tap ⬥, enter your current location and your destination, and then tap a method of transport (car, public transit, bicycle, or on foot) to see available routes.

- **Check Detailed Operation for Maps**: From the Maps app, tap **Menu** ≡ > **Help**.

Google Play Movies & TV

Google Play Movies & TV allows you to watch movies and TV shows purchased on Google Play. You can stream instantly on your Android phone or download so you can watch from anywhere, even when you are not connected. Also, get quick access to your personal video collection, including those taken on your phone.

Learn more about Google Play Movies & TV at play.google.com/about/movies.

- From home, tap **Apps** ⊞ > **Google** 🌐 > **Play Movies & TV** ▦.

Google Play Music

The Google Play Music app lets you browse, shop, and play back songs purchased from Google Play as well as songs you have loaded from your own music library. The music you choose is automatically stored in your Google Play Music library and instantly ready to play by streaming or download.

Note: For information about loading music onto your phone, see Transfer Files Between Your Phone and a Computer.

Using Google Play Music

Use the Google Play Music app to listen to all your music on your phone. Compatible music file formats include: MP3 (.mp3), AAC (m4a), WMA (.wma), FLAC (.flac), OGG (.ogg), DRM protected AAC (m4p), and ALAC (.m4a).

1. From home, tap **Apps** ⊞ > **Play Music** 🎧.

* The Play Music app opens to the Listen Now screen. To view additional music options, tap **Menu** ≡ and select an option (My Library, Playlists, Instant Mixes, or Shop).

2. Tap an item from the category window and then tap a song.

* The song begins playing.

Note: The first time you access Google Play Music, you may see a series of introductory screens. Tap **Listen now** to continue to the app.

Google Play Music Screen Layout

The following diagram outlines the main features of the Play Music app player screen.

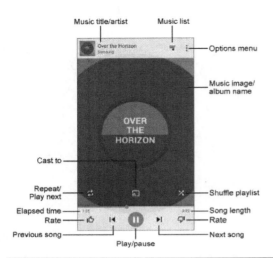

Music title/artist   Music list

Options menu

Music image/
album name

Cast to

Repeat/
Play next

Shuffle playlist

Elapsed time   Song length
Rate   Rate
Previous song   Next song
Play/pause

Feature	Description
Music list	View current playlist or queue
Options menu	Access the options menu.
Music image/album name	Display music images and album names (if available).
Shuffle playlist	Shuffle the current playlist or queue.
Song length	The length of the song.
Rate (thumbs up/thumbs down)	Rate the current song.
Next song	Play the next song.
Play/pause	Play or pause the current song.
Previous song	Play the previous song.
Elapsed time	Amount of time the song has been playing.
Repeat/play next	Repeat the current song or play the next song queued.
Cast to	Cast the song to a connected device.
Music title/artist	Displays music title and artist (if available).

Apps and Features

Create Playlists in Google Play Music

Organize music into playlists to fit every occasion.

1. From home, tap **Apps** 🔢 > **Play Music** 🎧.

❖ The Play Music app opens to the Listen Now screen.

2. Tap **Menu** ≡ to view your library or playlists, or to access Google Play Music online.

3. From a list displaying songs, tap **More options** ⋮ next to a song you want to add to a playlist.

4. Tap **Add to playlist** > **New playlist**.

5. Enter a Name, Description, and accessibility option for the playlist, and then tap **Create playlist**.

6. To add more songs, tap **More options** ⋮ next to a song and then tap **Add to playlist** > **[playlist name]**.

Adding Currently Playing Music to a Playlist

■ From the player view, tap **More options** ⋮ > **Add to playlist** and then tap the name of a playlist.

❖ The music is added to the playlist.

Google Search

Search information saved on the phone and in phone applications as well as on the Internet.

Use Google Search

Type search terms in the Google Search bar to find information on your phone and around the globe.

1. From home, tap the Google search bar or tap **Apps** ▦ > **Google** ● > **Google** Ⓖ.

❖ The Search window opens.

▪ If a description for Google Now appears, tap **What can Google Now do?** and read the information. Tap **Get started** on the last page if you want to use Google Now, or tap **Skip** to continue to the Google search page.

2. Type your search keywords and tap **Search** 🔍.

❖ Search results appear.

- To search by voice, tap 🎤 in the search bar and speak your search terms.

Google Search Options

- **Changing Search Information**: In the search results window, tap **Menu** ☰ > **Settings** > **Phone search** and select where to search.

- **Using Google Now**: Google Now automatically searches for information based on search keywords used, your current location, and more, and presents search results in the search screen. Google Now also informs users of scheduled events.

  - To enable Google Now, in the search results window, tap **Menu** ☰ > **Settings**. Tap **Now cards**, and then tap **ON/OFF** next to Show cards.

  - To disable Google Now, in the search results window, tap **Menu** ☰ > **Settings**. Tap **Now cards**, and then tap **ON/OFF** next to Show cards. Tap **Turn off** to confirm.

Use Google Voice Search

Use your voice to search instead of typing, with Google Voice Search.

1. From home, tap **Apps** ⊞ > **Google** 🔵 > **Voice Search** 🎤.

   ❖ The Voice Search window opens.

2. Speak your search terms.

   ❖ Search results appear.

Instagram

Capture and share photos and videos with your friends. Customize what you capture, and then share it on your feed or post it directly to your friends. Located in the Social folder in the apps list.

Install Instagram

1. From home, tap **Apps** ⊞ > **Instagram** 📷.

2. Tap **Download**, and then follow the prompts to accept access requirements and update the app.

Use Instagram

- From home, tap **Apps** ⊞ > **Instagram** 📷.

    - The first time you access Instagram, follow the prompts to sign up for an account, or sign in with Facebook or an existing account.

Memo

Use your phone's memo app to save text, memos, lists, and more.

1. From home, tap **Apps** ⊞ > **Tools** 🔧 > **Memo** 📝.

❖ The memo list appears.

2. Tap  and enter your memo title and text.

3. Tap **Save**.

   ❖ The memo is saved.

Messaging Plus

Messaging Plus provides high quality video calling, group chat, and media sharing along with easy registration, a full emoji keyboard, and other convenient features.

- From home, tap **Apps** ⊞ > **Messaging** .

Note: You can assign Messaging Plus as your phone's default messaging app, or as a standalone IM app. If you set Messaging Plus as the default messaging app, the Messages app will be disabled. For more information, see Default Messaging App Settings.

Messenger

Send instant messages with all your friends using Facebook's Messenger app.

Install Messenger

1. From home, tap **Apps** ⊞ > **Messenger** .

2. Tap **Download**, and then follow the prompts to accept access requirements and update the app.

Use Messenger

1. From home, tap **Apps** ⊞ > **Messenger** .

2. Follow the prompts to log in with your Facebook account. See Facebook.

Microsoft Excel

Create and share spreadsheets quickly and easily with Microsoft Excel.

- From home, tap **Apps** ▦ > **Microsoft Apps** ▦ > **Excel** 🗔.

Note: The first time you access Microsoft Excel on your phone, you may be prompted to update the app using Google Play. Follow the prompts to update and install the app.

Microsoft OneDrive

Microsoft OneDrive gives you free online storage for all your personal files so you can get to them from your Android device, computer, and any other devices you use.

- From home, tap **Apps** ▦ > **Microsoft Apps** ▦ > **OneDrive** ☁.

Note: The first time you access Microsoft OneDrive on your phone, you may be prompted to update the app using Google Play. Follow the prompts to update and install the app.

Microsoft OneNote

Stay organized using text, pictures, or audio notes with Microsoft. Create Quick Notes or review and edit shared OneNote notebooks.

- From home, tap **Apps** ▦ > **Microsoft Apps** ▦ > **OneNote** 🗔.

Note: The first time you access Microsoft OneNote on your phone, you may be prompted to update the app using Google Play. Follow the prompts to update and install the app.

Microsoft PowerPoint

Create and share presentations quickly and easily with Microsoft PowerPoint.

- From home, tap **Apps** ▦ > **Microsoft Apps** ▦ > **PowerPoint** 🗔.

Note: The first time you access Microsoft PowerPoint on your phone, you may be prompted to update the app using Google Play. Follow the prompts to update and install the app.

Microsoft Word

Create and share word processing documents quickly and easily with Microsoft Word.

- From home, tap **Apps** ▦ > **Microsoft Apps** ▦ > **Word** 🗔.

Note: The first time you access Microsoft Word on your phone, you may be prompted to update the app using Google Play. Follow the prompts to update and install the app.

My Files

My Files allows you to manage your sounds, images, videos, Bluetooth files, Android files, and other data in one convenient location. This application allows you to launch a file if the associated application is already on your phone.

1. From home, tap **Apps** ⊞ > **Tools** ▦ > **My Files** ▦.

2. Folders display, including:

   ▪ **Recent files**: View recently saved files. (Only appears if a file has been accessed recently.)

   ▪ **Images**: View image files.

   ▪ **Videos**: View video files.

   ▪ **Audio**: View audio files.

   ▪ **Documents**: View document files.

   ▪ **Download history**: View all apps and files that have been downloaded to the phone.

   ▪ **Local storage**: View folders and files in their storage locations.

Note: Different folders may appear depending on how your phone is configured.

To view files in My Files:

1. From home, tap **Apps** ⊞ > **Tools** ▦ > **My Files** ▦.

2. Tap a category to view its files or folders.

3. Tap a file or folder to open it.

NextRadio

NextRadio is an FM tuner application that receives FM radio broadcasts in your local area. NextRadio also provides a data service for radio broadcasters to share information about their station and their broadcast content so that listeners can receive real-time updates as they listen.

■ From home, tap **Apps** ⊞ > **NextRadio** ◉.

Note: To listen to radio from your device, you must plug in either headphones or a speaker cable to the headphone jack on top of the device. To listen through the device's speaker (after plugging in headphones), tap ▤ **More options** > **Output to speaker**.

Pages Manager

The Pages Manager app lets you manage up to 50 Pages from your smartphone or tablet. You can check Page activity, share with your audience and see insights.

Install Pages Manager

1. From home, tap **Apps** ⊞ > **Pages Manager** ▆.

2. Tap **Download**, and then follow the prompts to accept access requirements and update the app.

Use Pages Manager

- From home, tap **Apps** ⊞ > **Pages Manager** ▆.

Samsung Milk Music

Samsung Milk Music is a streaming radio service that offers a simple way to find the music that is right for you. With a library of over 13 million songs and 200+ stations, the interactive dial makes it easy to skim through stations, to find the perfect soundtrack for the moment.

1. From home, tap **Apps** ⊞ > **Samsung Milk Music** ♫.

2. Read the Terms and Conditions and Privacy Policy, and then tap **I agree** to continue.

3. Rotate the dial to select a music genre, and then tap ▶ to begin listening.

Tip: To stop listening and exit Samsung Milk Music, drag down the status bar to display the notification panel, and then tap ✕ next to the current song.

Uber

Search and find transportation service using the Uber app. Request a ride and get picked up within minutes.

Install Uber

1. From home, tap **Apps** ⊞ > **Uber** ▣.

2. Tap **Get started**, and then follow the prompts to update the app from the Google Play store.

Use Uber

- From home, tap **Apps** ⊞ > **Uber** ▣.

Video

Play videos stored on your phone, or from your other devices (you must sign in to your Samsung account to play videos synced from your other devices).

1. From home, tap **Apps** ⊞ > **Video** ▶.

2. Scroll through the videos stored on your phone. After a few seconds, each video thumbnail begins playing a preview of the clip.

3. Tap a video to view it.

Voice Recorder

The Voice recorder allows you to record an audio file up to one minute long and then immediately share it. Recording time will vary based on the available memory within the phone.

Make a Voice Recording

1. From home, tap **Apps** ▦ > **Tools** ▦ > **Voice Recorder** ◉.

2. Use the Voice Recorder controls:

- To start recording, tap **Record** ◉ and speak into the microphone.

- To pause recording, tap **Pause** ▮▮.

- To resume a paused recording tap **Resume** ◉.

- To end the recording, tap **Stop** ◻.

- To cancel the recording, tap **Back** ⬑, and then tap **Discard**.

- To block incoming calls while recording, tap **Call rejection** ▨.

Play Back a Voice Recording

1. From a home screen, **Apps** ▦ > **Tools** ▦ > **Voice Recorder** ◉.

2. Tap **Recordings** .

3. Tap a recording to play it back.

Share a Voice Recording

1. From home, tap **Apps** > **Tools** > **Voice Recorder** .

2. Tap **Recordings** , and then touch and hold on a recording to display options.

3. Tap **More** > **Share**, and then follow the prompts to choose a method and share the file.

Rename a Voice Recording

1. From home, tap **Apps** > **Tools** > **Voice Recorder** .

2. Tap **Recordings** , and then touch and hold on a recording to select it.

3. Tap **More** > **Rename** to change the name of the voice recording.

Voice Recorder Options

1. From home, tap **Apps** > **Tools** > **Voice Recorder** .

2. Tap **Recordings** to view a list of recordings.

3. Tap **More** for options:

   - **Edit**: Tap on recordings to select them. After selection, you can delete or rename the recordings.

   - **Share**: Select voice recordings to share.

Delete a Voice Recording

1. From home, tap **Apps** ⊞ > **Tools** 🔘 > **Voice Recorder** 🔘.

2. Tap **Recordings** ▤, and then touch and hold on a recording to select it.

3. Tap **Delete** > **Delete**.

YouTube

View videos uploaded to YouTube and upload your own videos to your YouTube account.

View YouTube Videos

You can use the YouTube app to view videos on YouTube even if you aren't signed in to a YouTube account.

1. From home, tap **Apps** ⊞ > **YouTube** ▶.

   ❖ The YouTube app launches.

2. Search through the YouTube channels and tap a video you want to see.

   ❖ The video plays on your phone screen.

   ▪ Tap the screen to pause or resume play while watching.

Post a Video to YouTube

You can post videos to your YouTube account from your phone. Before posting, you must set up a YouTube account and sign in to it on your phone.

1. From home, tap **Apps** ⊞ > **YouTube** ▶.

   ❖ The YouTube app launches.

2. Tap **Account** 🖼.

   ❖ Your account menu appears.

3. Tap **Upload** 🔘 to select a video from your phone.

   ▪ Enter a title, description, and tags, and select a privacy setting.

4. Tap **Upload** ▷.

   ❖ The video is uploaded to your YouTube channel.

Connectivity

The following topics address your phone's connectivity options, including USB file transfer and tethering, Wi-Fi, Bluetooth, IR connectivity, and more.

Transfer Files Between Your Phone and a Computer

You can use the supplied USB connector to connect your phone directly to your computer and transfer music, pictures, and other content files.

For example, if you have a music album stored on your computer that you want to listen to on your phone with any of the music apps, just attach your phone to the computer and copy the files to the music folder.

Data exchange may use the methods outlined in the following table:

Method	Description
Media device (MTP)	Transfer files between your phone and PC such as pictures, videos, and music.
Camera (PTP)	Transfer picture and video files between your phone and PC.
Mass storage mode	Exchange data with a PC using your phone as an external storage device.

Transfer Files Between the Phone and a Computer

1. Connect your phone to your computer using the supplied USB/charging cable.

- Insert the cable to the charger/accessory port at the bottom of the phone.

- Insert the USB end of the cable into an available USB port on your computer. You may need to remove the USB cable from the charging head to access it.

Note: The first time you attach the phone to a computer, the device driver software will automatically install on the computer.

2. Drag the status bar down to display the notification panel.

3. You will see either **Connected as a media device** or **Connected as a camera**.

   - The files on your phone can now be accessed using your computer.

   - For most transfers, you will want to use **Connected as a media device**.

   - To change the option, tap the notification in the notification panel to open the **USB computer connection** window, and then tap the desired option.

4. On your computer, navigate to the detected device (such as through the My Computer menu) and open it.

5. Select **Phone** for internal phone storage.

6. Select a folder (for example, **Music** for songs and albums) and copy files to it from your computer.

7. When you are done, disconnect your phone from your computer.

   ❖ The transferred files are now saved to your phone.

Note: You can also copy files from your phone to your computer, for example, if you want to save pictures or videos from your phone on your computer.

Wi-Fi

Wi-Fi provides wireless Internet access over distances of up to 300 feet. To use your phone's Wi-Fi, you need access to a wireless access point or "hotspot."

The availability and range of the Wi-Fi signal depends on a number of factors, including infrastructure and other objects through which the signal passes.

Turn Wi-Fi On and Connect to a Wireless Network

Use the Connections setting menu to enable your phone's Wi-Fi feature and connect to an available Wi-Fi network.

1. From home, tap **Apps** 🔲 > **Settings** ⚙️ > **Wi-Fi** 📶.

   ❖ The Wi-Fi settings menu appears.

2. Tap **ON/OFF** to turn Wi-Fi on.

   ❖ Wi-Fi is enabled. You will see the names and security settings of in-range Wi-Fi networks.

- To disable Wi-Fi, tap **ON/OFF** again.

3. Tap a Wi-Fi network to connect, enter the password (if it is not an open network), and then tap **Connect**.

- ❖ Your phone is connected to the Wi-Fi network. You will see 📶 in the status bar.

- The password, for a household wireless LAN router, is sometimes found on a sticker on the router (WEP, WPA, KEY, and more). Contact the router manufacturer for information. For password for a public wireless LAN, check with the user's service provider.

- Entering a password is not required if an access point is not security protected.

Note: The next time your phone connects to a previously accessed secured wireless network, you will not be prompted to enter the password again, unless you reset your phone to its factory default settings or you instruct the phone to forget the network.

Wi-Fi Settings

Use the Wi-Fi settings menu to manually set your Wi-Fi connection options.

1. From home, tap **Apps**  > **Settings** > **Wi-Fi** .

   ❖ The Wi-Fi settings menu appears.

2. Tap **ON/OFF** to turn Wi-Fi on.

   ❖ Wi-Fi is enabled. You will see the names and security settings of in-range Wi-Fi networks.

   ▪ To disable Wi-Fi, tap **ON/OFF** again.

3. Tap **More** > **Advanced**.

❖ The advanced Wi-Fi settings menu appears.

4. Configure your Wi-Fi settings.

❖ Your Wi-Fi settings changes are saved.

Disconnect Wi-Fi

You may want to remove a connected Wi-Fi network.

1. From home, tap **Apps** ▦ > **Settings** ⚙ > **Wi-Fi** 📶.

❖ The Wi-Fi settings menu appears.

2. Press and hold the name of the connected access point, and then tap **Forget network**.

   ❖ Wi-Fi is disconnected and the network settings are removed.

   ▪ After "forgetting" an access point, you need to enter the correct password (and other network settings, if required) to reconnect.

Wi-Fi Direct

Use Wi-Fi Direct to connect directly to other Wi-Fi Direct devices using only Wi-Fi, without a wireless access point (network) or using the Internet.

1. From home, tap **Apps** ⊞ > **Settings** ⊙ > **Wi-Fi** 📶.

   ❖ The Wi-Fi settings menu appears.

2. Tap **ON/OFF** to turn Wi-Fi on.

❖ Wi-Fi is enabled. You will see the names and security settings of in-range Wi-Fi networks.

3. Tap **Wi-Fi Direct**.

❖ The Wi-Fi Direct settings menu appears.

▪ Wi-Fi Direct and Wi-Fi are unavailable at the same time.

4. If a device is found, tap the device entry to connect.

▪ If connected using Wi-Fi, you will see a confirmation. Follow the prompts.

5. Accept the connection on the other device.

❖ The phone is connected using Wi-Fi Direct.

- If a connection is not accepted after a certain period, the connection request is cancelled.

- To stop a connection, tap the device name on the Wi-Fi Direct list.

Bluetooth

Bluetooth is a short-range communications technology that allows you to connect wirelessly to a number of Bluetooth devices, such as headsets and hands-free car kits, and Bluetooth-enabled handhelds, computers, printers, and wireless phones. The Bluetooth communication range is usually approximately 30 feet.

Bluetooth Hints

Problem: I cannot use Bluetooth.

Solution: Is your phone in Airplane mode? Bluetooth is unavailable in Airplane mode.

⚠ Bluetooth Function Cautions

Information may not appear correctly on connected devices depending on the transferred data.

Bluetooth Information

Bluetooth is a technology that enables wireless connection with PCs, Bluetooth devices with hands-free features, and more.

Function	Description
Audio output	Listen to music and more, wirelessly.
Hands-free calls	Call hands-free, using Bluetooth-capable hands-free devices and headsets.
Data exchange	Exchange data with Bluetooth devices.

Enable Bluetooth

Use the settings menu to enable or disable your phone's Bluetooth capabilities.

- Wireless connection to all Bluetooth functions is not guaranteed for the phone.

- The phone may not connect properly depending on the other device.

- Noise may be experienced with wireless calls and hands-free calls depending on the conditions.

To enable Bluetooth:

1. From home, tap **Apps** > **Settings** > **Bluetooth**.

   ❖ The Bluetooth settings open.

2. Tap **ON/OFF** to turn Bluetooth on.

   ❖ Bluetooth is enabled.

   ▪ To disable Bluetooth, tap **ON/OFF** again.

Tip: You can also turn Bluetooth on or off with the Quick settings button in the notification panel. Drag the status bar down to display the notification panel and then tap **Bluetooth** to turn Bluetooth on or off.

Note: Turn off Bluetooth when not in use to conserve battery power, or in places where using a wireless phone is prohibited, such as aboard an aircraft and in hospitals.

Pair Bluetooth Devices

Search for and pair nearby Bluetooth devices. Saved Bluetooth devices can be connected simply.

Note: Before pairing, turn on Bluetooth on the other device and make sure it is visible or discoverable.

To pair Bluetooth devices:

1. From home, tap **Apps** ▦ > **Settings** ⚙ > **Bluetooth** ✦.

   ❖ The Bluetooth settings open.

   ▪ Nearby devices that are visible or discoverable appear in the Available devices list.

   ▪ If a target device is not detected, tap **Scan** to search again.

2. Tap a device from the Available devices list, and follow the prompts to pair with the device. Methods to accept a Bluetooth connection differ depending on the device used.

❖ The Bluetooth device is paired to your phone.

Unpairing from a Paired Device

1. From the Bluetooth settings menu, tap **Settings** ⚙ next to the paired device you wish to unpair.

2. Tap **Unpair**.

❖ The device is unpaired from your phone. To make another connection with the device, you will need to pair again.

Connect to a Paired Bluetooth Device

You can listen to music over a Bluetooth stereo headset, or have hands-free conversations using a compatible Bluetooth headset or car kit. It is the same procedure to set up stereo audio and hands-free devices.

1. From home, tap **Apps** ⊞ > **Settings** ⚙ > **Bluetooth** ✳.

   ❖ The Bluetooth settings open.

   ▪ Paired Bluetooth devices appear in the Paired devices list.

2. Tap a device from the Paired devices list.

   ❖ Your phone connects to the paired device.

Connectivity 231

The pairing and connection status is displayed below the device's name in the Bluetooth devices section.

When the device is connected to your phone, the Bluetooth connected icon ⚹ is displayed in the status bar. Depending on the type of device you have connected, you can then start using the headset or car kit to listen to music or make and receive phone calls.

Note: Due to different specifications and features of other Bluetooth-compatible devices, display and options may be different, and functions such as transfer or exchange may not be possible with all Bluetooth-compatible devices.

Share Information Using Bluetooth

You can use Bluetooth to transfer information between your phone and another Bluetooth-enabled device such as a phone or notebook computer.

Types of Data You Can Send Using Bluetooth

You can send the following types of information, depending on the device you are sending to:

- Images and videos
- Calendar events
- Contacts
- Audio files

The instructions below illustrate sharing information using Bluetooth by describing how to share a contact.

Sending Contacts Data Using Bluetooth

Note: Your phone must be paired with another Bluetooth-enabled device in order to send information.

1. From home, tap **Apps** 🔳 > **Contacts** 👤.

❖ You will see the Contacts list.

2. Tap a contact to send.

3. Tap **More** > **Share contact** > **Bluetooth**.

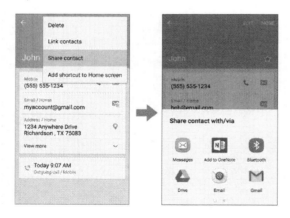

4. Tap a paired device to receive the data.

❖ The contact information is sent.

▪ If you see a message to confirm, follow the prompts.

Receiving Data Using Bluetooth

Transfer files to your device using Bluetooth.

Note: Your phone must be paired with another Bluetooth-enabled device in order to send information.

1. When another device attempts to send a file to your phone using Bluetooth, you will see a request to accept the file.

2. Tap **Accept**.

❖ The file is sent to your phone.

▪ When your phone receives a file, you will see a notification. To open the file immediately, drag the status bar down to display the notification panel, and then tap the notification.

- When you open a received file, what happens next depends on the file type:

  - Media files and documents are usually opened directly in a compatible application.

  - For a vCalendar file, select the calendar where you want to save the event, and then tap **Import**. The vCalendar is added to your Calendar events. (For more information on using the Calendar, see Calendar.)

  - For a vCard contact file, received contacts are stored in the Contacts list.

Settings

The following topics provide an overview of items you can change using your phone's **Settings** menus.

Basic Settings

From home, tap **App** ⊞ > **Settings** ⚙ to access your phone's settings menu.

The table below outlines the top-level settings categories.

Category	Description
Wi-Fi	Enable and set Wi-Fi options.
Bluetooth	Enable Bluetooth connections.
Mobile Hotspot	Use the Mobile Hotspot feature to share your phone's data connection with other devices using Wi-Fi.
Airplane mode	Turn Airplane mode on or off.
Data usage	Check your phone's data usage.
Mobile networks	View and configure your mobile network connections and settings.
More connection settings	Set wireless and network functions, including selecting a default messaging app, printing services, and setting up a Virtual Private Network (VPN).
Sounds and notifications	Set ringtone, notification tones, and more.
Display	Set display features, font, brightness, and more.
Motions and gestures	Enable phone controls by using motions and gestures.
Applications	Manage applications, default apps, and system processes.
Wallpaper	Set wallpaper for the home and lock screens.
Themes	Select visual themes for your phone.
Lock screen and security	Set your phone's lock screen options. Set security features such as device administrators, encryption, and trusted credentials.
Privacy	Configure privacy features, including location method.

Category	Description
Easy mode	Enable Easy mode for your phone, simplifying the layout and interface.
Accessibility	Set accessibility options such as screen magnification, hearing aid compatibility, and more.
Accounts	Set up accounts such as Samsung, Google, and more.
Backup and reset	Set up backup options for your phone, as well as resetting the phone to its factory defaults.
Language and input	Set up Language and input methods for your phone.
Battery	Display the battery charge as a percentage on the status bar, view battery usage by application and system process, and configure power saving modes.
Storage	View total and available system memory.
Date and time	Set your phone's date and time.
Activate this device	Activate your device with the Boost network.
System Update	Update your system's software, PRL, and Profile.
About device	View device status, legal information, and hardware information about your device.

Access Settings

- From home, tap **Apps** 🎛 > **Settings** 🔘.

  – or –

Slide the status bar down to open the notification panel, and then tap **Settings** ⚙.

❖ The settings menu opens.

Customize Quick Settings

At the top of the main settings menu is a section of Quick settings. You can include up to nine primary settings options in the Quick settings menu.

To customize Quick settings:

1. From home, tap **Apps** ⊞ > **Settings** ⚙.

2. Tap **Edit**.

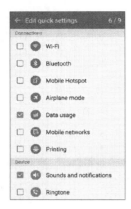

3. Check or uncheck options to include in Quick settings. The counter at the top right corner indicates how many items have been selected out of the maximum of 9.

4. Tap the **Back** key ⤺ to return to the main settings menu.

Wi-Fi Settings Menu

The Wi-Fi settings menu lets you turn Wi-Fi on or off, set up and connect to available Wi-Fi networks, and configure advanced Wi-Fi options.

For more information about using Wi-Fi, see Wi-Fi.

1. From home, tap **Apps** ⊞ > **Settings** ⚙ > **Wi-Fi** 📶.

❖ The Wi-Fi settings menu appears.

2. Tap **ON/OFF** to turn Wi-Fi on.

❖ Wi-Fi is enabled. You will see the names and security settings of in-range Wi-Fi networks.

▪ To disable Wi-Fi, tap **ON/OFF** again.

3. Tap a Wi-Fi network, enter the password, and tap **Connect**.

❖ Your phone is connected to the selected Wi-Fi network.

▪ The password, for a household wireless LAN router, is sometimes found on a sticker on the router (WEP, WPA, KEY, and more). Contact the router manufacturer for information. For password for a public wireless LAN, check with user's service provider.

▪ Entering a password is not required if an access point is not security protected.

Connect to a Wi-Fi Network Using WPS

Wi-Fi Protected Setup (WPS) is a network security standard that allows you to easily secure a wireless network connection between your phone and a router.

To connect using a WPS button:

1. From Wi-Fi settings, tap **More** > **WPS push button**.

2. Tap the WPS button on your router.

3. Follow the prompts to complete the connection.

To connect using a Personal Identification Number (PIN):

1. From Wi-Fi settings, tap **More** > **WPS PIN entry**.

2. Enter the PIN displayed on your router.

3. Follow the prompts to complete the connection.

Smart Network Switch

Smart network switch lets your phone automatically switch to the wireless network data connection when the current Wi-Fi connection is unstable.

1. From the Wi-Fi settings menu, tap **More** > **Smart network switch**.

2. Tap **On** to enable the feature.

Advanced Wi-Fi Settings

The advanced Wi-Fi settings menu lets you set up and manage wireless access points.

■ From the Wi-Fi menu, tap **More** > **Advanced** to access the advanced Wi-Fi settings:

  ▪ **Network notification**: Tap **ON/OFF** to enable notification when open networks are available.

  ▪ **Passpoint**: Tap **ON/OFF** to enable automatic connection to Passpoint-certified Wi-Fi access points.

  ▪ **Keep Wi-Fi on during sleep**: Select options for keeping Wi-Fi active while the phone is sleeping.

  ▪ **Always allow scanning**: Tap **ON/OFF** to enable or disable background scanning even when Wi-Fi is turned off.

  ▪ **Install network certificates**: Install security certificates from your phone storage.

  ▪ **MAC address**: View your phone's MAC address.

  ▪ **IP address**: View the phone's IP address.

Bluetooth Settings

Your phone's Bluetooth capabilities let you use wireless headsets, send and receive pictures and files, and more. For details on your phone's Bluetooth usage, see Bluetooth.

Access Bluetooth Settings

- From home, tap **Apps** ⊞ > **Settings** ⚙ > **Bluetooth** ❊.

❖ The Bluetooth settings open.

Bluetooth Settings Options

- **Enable Bluetooth**: In Bluetooth settings, tap **ON/OFF** to enable.

  - When enabled, confirmation appears for your phone to be discoverable by other devices. Follow the prompts.

- **Pairing Bluetooth devices**: Make sure the other devices are set to be discovered. From Bluetooth settings, tap the device name in Available devices and follow the prompts.

  - Depending on the device, you may be required to enter or accept a passkey.

  - If the target device does not appear, tap **Scan** to search again.

  - This setting is available when Bluetooth is enabled.

- **Change the name of a paired device**: From Bluetooth settings, tap **Settings** ⚙ next to a paired device name, tap **Rename**, enter a new name, and tap **Rename**.

  - Emoji cannot be used in a device name.

  - This setting is available when Bluetooth is enabled.

- **Cancelling pairing**: From Bluetooth settings, tap **Settings** ⚙ next to a paired device name, and then tap **Unpair**.

  - This setting is available when Bluetooth is enabled.

- **Enable service from paired device**: From Bluetooth settings, tap **Settings** ⚙ next to a paired device name, and then tap the listing under **Use for**.

  - If a confirmation prompt appears, follow the prompts.

  - This setting is available when Bluetooth is enabled.

  - This setting is available when the paired device is providing a service.

  - Tap **ON/OFF** to turn the option on.

- **Search for other devices**: From Bluetooth settings, tap **Scan**.

  - This setting is available when Bluetooth is enabled.

- **Check files received using Bluetooth transfer**: From Bluetooth settings, tap **More** > **Received files**, and then follow the prompts.

Hotspot Settings

Use the Hotspot feature to share your phone's data connection with other devices using Wi-Fi.

Important: Use of the Hotspot feature requires an additional subscription. Visit boostmobile.com to learn more.

Note: Using the Hotspot feature consumes battery power and uses data services.

Turn Hotspot On or Off

To conserve battery life, turn Hotspot on when you need it and turn it off when you are finished. You can control Hotspot from Settings.

1. From home, tap **Apps** ⊞ > **Settings** ⚙ > **Mobile Hotspot** ⊕.

❖ The Hotspot settings open.

2. Tap **ON/OFF** to turn Hotspot on or off.

Note: Turning on Hotspot will turn off Wi-Fi.

Configure Hotspot

Set up Hotspot to your preferences.

1. From home, tap **Apps** ⊞ > **Settings** ⚙ > **Mobile Hotspot** ⊕.

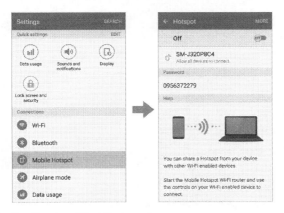

2. Tap **More** to set the following options:

- **Configure Hotspot:**
  - **Network name**: View and change the name of your Mobile Hotspot.
  - **Hide my device**: When enabled, your Mobile Hotspot is not visible to other Wi-Fi devices during a scan. Other devices can still connect to your Mobile Hotspot, but will have to set up the connection manually with your Network SSID and Password.
  - **Security**: Choose the security level for your Mobile Hotspot.
  - **Password**: If you choose a security level that uses a password, set a password.
  - **Show password**: When enabled, the contents of the Password field are visible.
  - **Show advanced options**: When enabled, you can access advanced options, including Broadcast channel, to specify the channel your device uses for the Mobile Hotspot, and you can set the maximum number of connections to your Mobile Hotspot.
- **Timeout settings**: Choose a time period, after which Mobile Hotspot will automatically turn off if there is no activity.
- **LAN settings**: View and configure settings related to using your Mobile Hotspot as a Local Area Network.
  - **IP address**: View the default IP address, or tap to enter a valid IPv4 address.
  - **Subnet mask**: View the default subnet mask, or tap to enter a subnet mask.
  - **DHCP**: Tap to enable or disable DHCP. When DHCP is enabled, your phone assigns IP addresses to devices that connect to Hotspot.
  - **Starting IP**: When DHCP is enabled, view the default starting IP address for assigning IP addresses to connecting devices, or enter a enter a valid IPv4 address. When other devices connect to your device using DHCP, the IP address your phone assigns will be between the Starting IP and Ending IP.
  - **Ending IP**: When DHCP is enabled, view the default ending IP address for assigning IP addresses to connecting devices, or enter a enter a valid IPv4 address. When other devices connect to your device using DHCP, the IP address your phone assigns will be between the Starting IP and Ending IP.
  - **Lease time**: When DHCP is enabled, set a length of time a connected device may use an assigned IP address.
  - **Maximum DHCP users**: When DHCP is enabled, set the maximum number of devices allowed to connect to your Hotspot.

Allowed Devices

Control whether devices can connect to your Mobile Hotspot with the Allowed devices list. After you add devices to the list, they can scan for your phone and connect using your phone's Hotspot name and password.

Note: Using the Hotspot feature consumes battery power and uses data services.

1. From home, tap **Apps** ⊞ > **Settings** ⚙ > **Mobile Hotspot** ⬤.

2. Tap **More** > **Allowed devices**.

3. Tap **Add**, and then enter the other device's **Device name** and **MAC address**. Consult the other device's settings to find these details.

4. Tap **OK** to add the device to the Allowed devices list.

Airplane Mode

When you enable Airplane mode, your phone disconnects from all networks, meaning you cannot use make calls, send or receive messages, or access the Internet. It also turns off other connectivity features, such as Wi-Fi and Bluetooth.

While in Airplane mode, you can use other features of your phone, such as playing music, watching videos, or other applications.

To use Wi-Fi and Bluetooth after enabling Airplane mode, turn them on either in Settings or on the notification panel.

1. From home, tap **Apps**  > **Settings** > **Airplane mode** .

2. Tap **ON/OFF** to enable Airplane mode.

Note: You can also enable or disable Airplane Mode through the notification panel Quick settings (drag down the status bar and tap **Airplane mode** > **Turn on**), or through the Power/Lock key (press and hold the **Power/Lock** key, and then tap **Airplane mode** > **Turn on**).

Data Usage Settings

The Data usage menu lets you view your phone's mobile and Wi-Fi data usage, set data limits, restrict Hotspot usage, and more.

- From home, tap **Apps** ■ > **Settings** ⚙ > **Data usage** 📊.

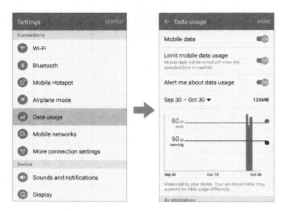

❖ The data usage window opens.

Data Usage Settings Options

- **Mobile data**: Tap **ON/OFF** next to **Mobile data**.

- **Limit mobile data usage**: Tap **ON/OFF** next to **Limit mobile data usage**, and then drag the horizontal limit slider up or down to set the data usage limit.

  - This setting is available when Mobile data is enabled.

- **Alert me about data usage**: Tap **ON/OFF** next to **Alert me about data usage**, and then drag the horizontal warning slider up and down to set an amount.

  - Data usage amounts are approximate. Actual amounts may differ.

  - This setting is available when Mobile data is enabled.

- **Set dates for data usage tracking**: Tap the date range to set the data usage measuring cycle.

  - This setting is available when Mobile data is enabled.

- **Application data usage**: Tap an app name to see its usage for the period.

- **More**: Tap **More** and select additional options:

  - **Restrict background data**: Prevent apps and services from using mobile data services unless connected to a Wi-Fi network.

  - **Show Wi-Fi usage**: Display a Wi-Fi tab at the top of the Data usage window. Tap the tab to view your phone's Wi-Fi data usage.

  - **Restrict networks.** Set apps to warn you before using these networks for large downloads.

Mobile Networks Settings

The Mobile networks settings menu allows you to configure your mobile network connections.

Set options for network selection and data service.

1. From home, tap **Apps** ▦ > **Settings** ⚙ > **Mobile networks** 🔘.

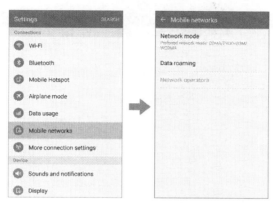

2. Configure options:

   - **Network mode**: Choose a preferred network mode. Available options depend on your phone's features, but may include: CDMA, LTE/CDMA, GSM/UMTS, and Automatic (the recommended setting).

   - **Data roaming**: When you are outside your home network area, your phone can still connect to other networks that your provider supports using roaming. There may be additional costs for accessing networks while roaming, so you may want to control your phone's roaming behavior with Roaming settings.

      - **Roaming network**: Select a roaming default. Choose **Home only**, to only connect to the Boost network, or **Automatic** to allow connections to Boost's partner networks, when available.

      - **Roaming guard**: Choose options for displaying a roaming notice for certain functions. Enable or disable roaming notices for Voice and Data for Domestic, Voice, Data and Outgoing text message for International networks, and Voice, Data and Outgoing text message for GSM networks (if supported by your phone).

   - **Network operators**: View mobile network operator information for international GSM networks.

More Connection Settings

The More connection settings menu provides access to additional network options, such as default messaging app, VPN, mobile networks, and printers (if available).

More Connection Settings Options

Setting	Description
Tethering	Share your device's mobile data connection using USB or Bluetooth.
Printing	Set up printers to print from your phone.
VPN	Add a Virtual Private Network (VPN).
Default messaging app	Set a default text messaging app.

Access More Connection Options

1. From home, tap **Apps** ⊞ > **Settings** ⚙ > **More connection settings** 🌐.

2. Set items.

   ❖ Your settings are saved and implemented.

Tethering Settings

Use Tethering to share your device's Internet connection with a computer that connects to your device using USB cable or by Bluetooth.

Important: Use of the Tethering feature requires an additional subscription. Visit boostmobile.com to learn more.

Note: Using the tethering feature consumes battery power and uses data services.

1. From home, tap **Apps** ⊞ > **Settings** ⚙ > **More connection settings** 📶.

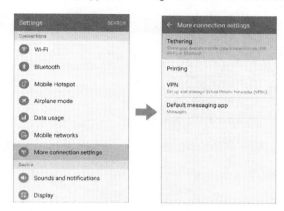

2. Tap **Tethering**.

- **Bluetooth tethering**: Pair your device with the computer using Bluetooth. Consult the computer's documentation for more information about configuring your computer to pair using Bluetooth. Tap **Bluetooth tethering** to turn tethering on.

Printing

You can print from your phone, using Wi-Fi, to an optional compatible printer (not included). Your phone and the optional printer must be connected to the same Wi-Fi network.

Add a Printer

Before you can print to a printer, you must add and set it up on your phone. You will need to know the IP address of the printer; consult the printer's documentation for this information.

1. From home, tap **Apps** ⊞ > **Settings** ⚙ > **More connection settings** ⚙ > **Printing**.

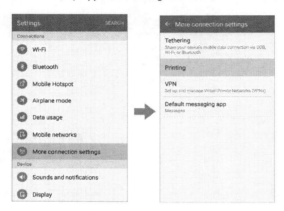

❖ The Printing settings screen displays.

2. From the Printing settings screen, tap **Download plug-in** ✚.

3. Follow the prompts to download and install a print driver from the Google Play store.

4. Choose a print service from the list, and then tap **ON/OFF** to turn the service on or off. The service must be on to add a printer.

5. Tap **More** > **Add printer** > **Add printer** (or ➕, depending on the plug-in), and then enter a name and the IP address of the printer.

Set Up a Printer

Add a printer to a print service and configure settings.

Note: Below settings are examples only. Available settings will differ depending on the type of print service and printer you are using.

1. From the Printing settings screen, select a print service from the list.

2. Tap **ON/OFF** to turn the service on. The service must be on to add a printer.

3. Tap **More** > **Add printer** and follow the prompts to add a printer.

4. Tap **More** > **Printer settings** to configure printer options. Available options may vary depending on the type of printer, and not all printers support all options.

Virtual Private Networks (VPN)

From your phone, you can add, set up, and manage virtual private networks (VPNs) that allow you to connect and access resources inside a secured local network, such as your corporate network.

Prepare Your Phone for VPN Connection

Depending on the type of VPN you are using at work, you may be required to enter your login credentials or install security certificates before you can connect to your company's local network. You can get this information from your network administrator.

Before you can initiate a VPN connection, your phone must first establish a Wi-Fi or data connection. For information about setting up and using these connections on your phone, see Browser and Turn Wi-Fi On and Connect to a Wireless Network.

Set Up Secure Credential Storage

If your network administrator instructs you to download and install security certificates, you must first set up the phone's secure credential storage.

1. From home, tap **Apps** 🎛 > **Settings** ⚙ > **Lock screen and security** 🔒.

2. Tap **Screen lock type** > **Password**.

Note: For credential storage, you can also use Pattern or PIN screen lock types. See Screen Lock.

3. Enter a new password (at least eight characters without any spaces) for the credential storage, scroll down and confirm the password, and then tap **OK**.

4. Select your display option for notifications on the lock screen, and then tap **Done**.

   ❖ The password is set, allowing secure credential storage.

5. On the Lock screen and security window, tap **Other security settings**.

6. Tap **Trust agents**, and then tap your preferred system and user credentials.

❖ Your secure credentials storage is set.

You can then download and install the certificates needed to access your local network. Your network administrator can tell you how to do this.

Add a VPN Connection

Use the More connection settings menu to add a VPN connection to your phone.

1. From home, tap **Apps** 🔳 > **Settings** ⚙ > **More connection settings** 🌐 > **VPN**.

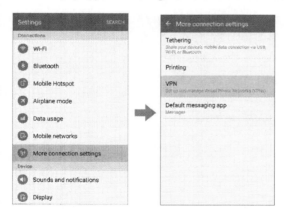

❖ The VPN settings window appears.

2. Tap **More** > **Add VPN**, and then enter the information for the VPN you want to add.

- Information may include Name, Type, Server address, PPP encryption (MPPE), and advanced options.

- Set up all options according to the security details you have obtained from your network administrator.

3. Tap **Save**.

❖ Your VPN is added to the VPNs section of the VPN settings window.

Access the VPN Settings Window

- From home, tap **Apps** ▦ > **Settings** ⚙ > **More connection settings** ● > **VPN**.

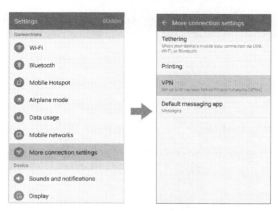

❖ The VPN settings window appears.

Connect to a VPN

1. From the VPNs section of the VPN setting window, tap the VPN that you want to connect to.

2. When prompted, enter your login credentials, and then tap **Connect**.

❖ You will connect to the selected VPN.

▪ When you are connected, a VPN connected icon appears in the notification area.

3. Open the Web browser to access resources such as intranet sites on your corporate network.

Disconnect from a VPN

1. Drag the status bar down to open the notification panel.

2. Tap the VPN connection to display the VPN connection window.

3. Tap **Disconnect** to disconnect from the VPN.

   ❖ Your phone disconnects from the VPN.

Default Messaging App Settings

If you have multiple messaging apps installed on your phone, you can choose the app your phone uses for messaging. The app you select here will be used when you choose Messages in other apps, such as when sharing items like pictures or video.

1. From home, tap **Apps** ⊞ > **Settings** ⚙ > **More connection settings** ⚙ > **Default messaging app**.

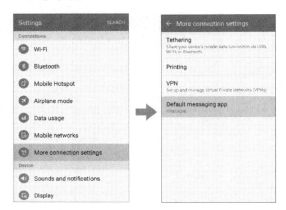

2. Choose a messaging app.

❖ The default messaging app is set.

Note: If you choose a default messaging app other than Messages (for example, Google Hangouts), you will not be able to use the standard Messages app unless you restore it as the default messaging app.

Sounds and Notifications Settings

The Sounds and notifications settings menu lets you control your phone's audio, from ringtones and alerts to tap tones and notifications.

Sounds and Notifications Settings Overview

The sounds and notifications settings menu allows you to configure the following options:

Sound Setting	Description
Sound mode	Set the sound mode for the phone (Sound, Vibrate, or Mute).
Volume	Set the volume for ringtones, media, system features, and more.
Ringtones and sounds	Set your ringtones and notification sounds for your phone, apps, keypad, and other features.
Vibrations	Configure vibration pattern, feedback, and other settings.
Sound quality and effects	Set sound quality and sound effects for your phone.
Do not disturb	Configure the Do not disturb feature to mute calls and alerts at will or on a schedule, as well as set exceptions.
Notifications on lock screen	Choose whether to display sensitive content and notifications when the screen is locked.
App notifications	Configure notifications for apps installed on your phone.

Sound Mode

You can switch between sound modes while preserving the individual sound settings you have made.

1. From home, tap **Apps** > **Settings** > **Sounds and notifications**.

2. Tap **Sound mode**, and then choose a mode:

- **Sound**: Your phone uses the sounds, vibrations, and volume levels you have chosen in Sound settings for notifications and alerts.

- **Vibrate**: Your phone vibrates for notifications and alerts.

- **Mute**: Your phone plays no sounds or vibrations. Reminders will still occur.

Volume

Set the system volume level, and set default volume for call ringtones, notifications, and other media.

Note: You can also set System volume from the home screen by pressing the **Volume** key.

1. From home, tap **Apps** ⊞ > **Settings** ⚙ > **Sounds and notifications** 🔊.

2. Tap **Volume** and then drag the sliders to set the default volume for:

- Ringtone

- Media

- Notifications

- System

Ringtones and Sounds

Choose a ringtone for incoming calls.

1. From home, tap **Apps** ⊞ > **Settings** ⚙ > **Sounds and notifications** 🔊.

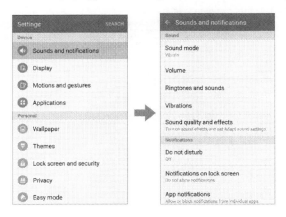

2. Tap **Ringtones and sounds** for options:

- **Ringtone**: Select a default ringtone.

- **Default notification sound**: Choose a default sound for notifications.

- **Messages notifications**: Tones play and/or the phone vibrates when new messages arrives.

- **Calendar notifications**: Tones play and/or the phone vibrates to remind you of events.

- **Email notifications**: Tones play and/or the phone vibrates when new emails arrive.

- **Touch sounds**: Tones play when you tap the screen to make selections.

- **Dialing keypad tone**: Tones play when you tap keys on the phone keypad.

- **Screen lock sounds**: Tones play when you tap the screen to lock or unlock it.

- **Emergency tone**: Select alert type for emergency notifications.

- **Keyboard sound**: Tones play when you tap the keyboard.

Add a Ringtone

When you select a ringtone, either from the settings menu or from Contacts, you can add a custom ringtone.

1. From the Ringtones and sounds menu, tap **Ringtone**.

2. Scroll to the bottom of the list and tap **Add ringtone** ✛.

3. Select a source (**OneDrive** or **Sound picker**) for the ringtone.

   ❖ You will see a list of compatible songs or audio files. To load music on your phone, see Transfer Files between Your Phone and a Computer.

4. Tap a song to hear a preview, and then tap **Done** to save it as a ringtone.

   ❖ The new ringtone is saved to the list and will be available to be assigned as a default ringtone or as a ringtone for individual contacts, groups, and more.

Vibrations

Choose vibrations to play for notifications, such as for incoming calls, new messages, and event reminders.

1. From home, tap **Apps** > **Settings** > **Sounds and notifications** .

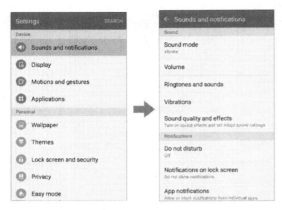

2. Tap **Vibrations** for options:

- **Vibration pattern**. Select a vibration pattern, or create a new one.

- **Vibrate while ringing**: The phone vibrates when ringing.

Sound Quality and Effects

Select options for sound quality while headphones or compatible Bluetooth headsets or speakers are connected.

1. From home, tap **Apps** > **Settings** > **Sounds and notifications** .

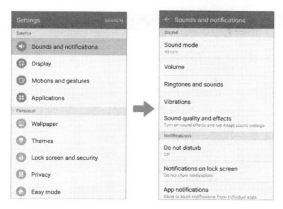

2. Tap **Sound quality and effects** for options:

- **Adapt Sound**: Find the best sound quality for you and use it during calls and while playing music or videos.

- **SoundAlive+**: Recreate the effect of rich surround sound.

- **Tube Amp**: Simulate the soft timbre of a tube amplifier.

Notifications

Choose a sound for notifications, such as for new messages and event reminders.

1. From home, tap **Apps** > **Settings** > **Sounds and notifications** .

2. Set notification sound options:

    - **Do not disturb**: Silence all calls and alerts during scheduled times. You can allow exceptions.

    - **Notifications on lock screen**: Choose whether to display sensitive content and notifications when the screen is locked.

    - **App notifications**: Allow or block notifications from individual apps.

Display Settings

Adjusting your phone's display and wallpaper settings not only helps you see what you want, it can also help increase battery life.

Display Settings Overview

The display settings menu allows you to configure the following options:

Display Setting	Description
Brightness	Set the display brightness.
Outdoor mode	Increase the screen brightness for 15 minutes to improve screen display for use outdoors.
Font	Set a default font and font size.

Display Setting	Description
Screen timeout	Set a screen timeout duration. Note: Longer durations discharge the battery more quickly
Screen mode	Select a screen display mode to optimize it for the content being displayed.
Daydream	Select a screensaver to be displayed when the device is docked or sleeping.

Access Display Settings

1. From home, tap **Apps** ⊞ > **Settings** ⚙ > **Display** ⬚.

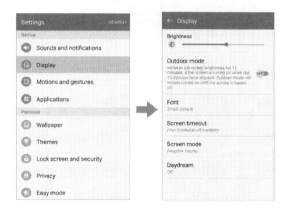

2. Set your display options:

   - **Brightness**: Set the screen brightness.

   - **Outdoor mode**: Increase the screen brightness for 15 minutes to improve screen display for use outdoors.

   - **Font**: Choose the default font.

   - **Screen timeout**: Turn the screen off after a set amount of time.

   - **Screen mode**: Adjust the screen display according to what is being displayed.

   - **Daydream**: Choose options for when the phone is docked or sleeping.

Motions and Gestures

Enable or disable motions and gestures which provide phone control by moving the phone or by gesturing.

Access Motions and Gestures Settings

1. From home, tap **Apps** ⚏ > **Settings** ◉ > **Motions and gestures** ⬤.

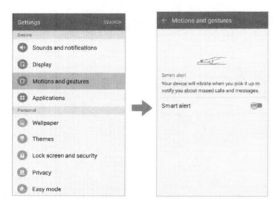

2. Tap **ON/OFF** to turn on Smart alert, which vibrates the phone when picked up to notify you about missed calls and messages.

Applications Settings

View information and configure settings for all apps on your phone. The Application manager and Default applications menus are located here.

Application Manager

Check installed applications and running applications. Items that can be checked in the Application manager are as follows:

Apps Setting	Description
Downloaded	Check downloaded apps.
SD Card	Check apps on the optional memory card (not included).
Running	Check running apps.

Apps Setting	Description
All	Check all apps.
Disabled	Check disabled apps. Tab is only available if you have disabled apps.

Access the Application Manager

1. From home, tap Apps ⊞ > Settings ⚙ > Applications ⊞.

2. Tap **Application manager**.

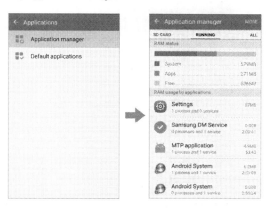

3. Tap items to view details.

❖ Check your application settings condition and access additional options.

Note: Depending on the app and its location, you may be able to force the app closed, uninstall or disable the app, clear cache and data, and more.

Default Applications

Set or clear default applications for certain built-in features of the phone.

1. From home, tap **Apps** ⊞ > **Settings** ⊚ > **Applications** ⊞.

2. Tap **Default applications**.

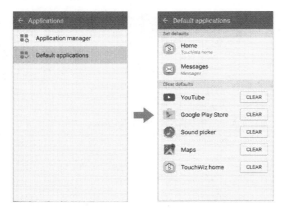

3. Tap each default setting to see what services or applications are available to set as the default.

- **Home**: Choose a default home screen mode.

- **Messages**: Choose a default app for messaging.

- **Clear defaults**: Tap **Clear** to clear any defaults you may have set during phone use, such as YouTube to view a video or Maps to launch a Web address link.

Note: If you choose a default messaging app other than Messages (Google Hangouts for example), you will not be able to use the Messages app unless you restore it as the default messaging app. For details, see Default Messaging App Settings.

Wallpaper

You can change the wallpaper for the Home and lock screens.

Change the Wallpaper

1. From home, tap **Apps** ⊞ > **Settings** ⚙ > **Wallpaper** ⊡.

2. Tap **Home screen** to open the drop-down list. Select the screens for which you want to change the wallpaper.

3. Tap a wallpaper to preview it.

4. Tap **Set as wallpaper** to set the selected wallpaper for the screen or screens.

   ❖ Your wallpaper is changed.

Themes

Themes are packages of visual content that provide different wallpapers and icons for your phone.

Change the Theme

1. From home, tap **Apps** ⊞ > **Settings** ⚙ > **Themes** ⬤.

– or –

Touch and hold an empty area on a home screen, and then tap **Themes**.

2. Tap a theme to view it.

3. To find other themes, tap **Theme store**.

4. To download a theme, tap the theme, and then tap **Download**.

5. To apply a theme, tap the theme, and then tap **Apply**.

    ❖ Your theme is changed.

Lock Screen and Security Settings

The lock screen settings let you set your method for unlocking your phone, customize lock screen options, determine whether to show tips for unlocking the phone, and enter your owner information to be displayed on the lock screen.

The Security settings let you set encryption options, password visibility, administrator settings, and credential storage options.

Lock Screen and Security Overview

The following options are available in the Lock screen and security menu (options vary depending on the screen lock selected):

Setting	Description
Screen lock type	Set your screen lock.

Setting	Description
Show information	Select items to show on the lock screen, like a Dual clock, the Weather, and Owner information.
Secure lock settings	Set your secure lock functions, such as Auto lock, and Lock instantly with the Power/Lock key.
Unlock effect	Set the effect shown when the lock screen wakes up.
Unknown sources	Allow or deny installation of apps from sources other than the Google Play store app.
Other security settings	Configure settings for encryption, password visibility, security updates, credentials, and other security features.

Access Lock Screen and Security Options

■ From home, tap **Apps** 🎛 > **Settings** ⚙ > **Lock screen and security** 🔒.

❖ The Lock screen and security menu opens.

Screen Lock

You can increase the security of your phone by creating a screen lock. When enabled, you have to draw the correct unlock pattern on the screen, enter the correct PIN, or enter the correct password to unlock the phone's control keys, buttons, and touchscreen.

In order from least secure to most secure, the available screen lock options are:

• Swipe

- Pattern

- PIN

- Password

- None

Important: To protect your phone and data from unauthorized access, it is recommended that you use the highest security level available (Password protection). It is also recommended you frequently change your password to ensure the safety of your phone and personal data.

Access Screen Lock Settings

1. From home, tap **Apps** ⊞ > **Settings** ⚙ > **Lock screen and security** 🔒.

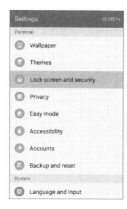

   ❖ The Lock screen and security menu opens.

2. Tap **Screen lock type**.

❖ The Screen lock settings menu opens.

Use Swipe to Unlock the Screen

■ From the Screen lock type menu, tap **Swipe** to save the setting.

❖ The screen lock is set.

Use a Screen Unlock Pattern

1. From the Screen lock type menu, tap **Pattern**.

2. Draw the screen unlock pattern by connecting at least four dots in a vertical, horizontal, or diagonal direction. Lift your finger from the screen when finished.

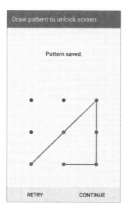

❖ The phone records the pattern.

3. Tap **Continue**.

4. When prompted, draw the screen unlock pattern again, and then tap **Confirm**.

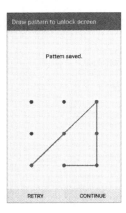

❖ The screen unlock pattern is saved.

5. Enter a backup PIN, tap **Continue**, re-enter the PIN, and tap **OK** to save your screen unlock pattern.

6. Select display options for notifications on the lock screen.

- ❖ The screen lock is set.

- If you fail to draw the correct unlock pattern on the screen after five attempts, you will be prompted to wait for 30 seconds before you can try again.

Note: If you do not want the unlock pattern to display on the screen when you unlock it, from home, tap **Apps** ⊞ > **Settings** ⚙ > **Lock screen and security** 🔒 > **Secure lock settings**, and then tap **ON/OFF** next to **Make pattern visible** to turn it off.

Note: To change your unlock screen pattern, from home, tap **Apps** ⊞ > **Settings** ⚙ > **Lock screen and security** 🔒 > **Screen lock type**.

Use a Screen Unlock PIN

1. From the Screen lock type menu, tap **PIN**.

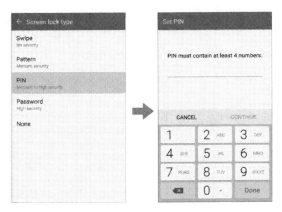

2. Enter a PIN, tap **Continue**, re-enter your PIN, and tap **OK** to save the setting.

3. Select display options for notifications on the lock screen.

❖ The screen lock is set.

▪ If you fail to enter the correct PIN after five attempts, you will be prompted to wait for 30 seconds before you can try again.

Use a Screen Unlock Password

1. From the Screen lock type menu, tap **Password**.

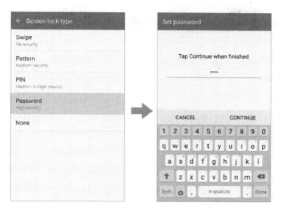

2. Enter a password with at least 4 characters, including at least one letter, tap **Continue**, and then enter your password again to confirm it.

3. Select display options for notifications on the lock screen.

❖ The screen lock is set.

▪ If you fail to enter the correct password after five attempts, you will be prompted to wait for 30 seconds before you can try again.

Important: To protect your phone and data from unauthorized access, it is recommended that you use the screen unlock password (highest security). It is also recommended that you frequently change your password to ensure the safety of your phone and personal data.

Disable the Screen Lock

Follow the instructions below to turn off your current screen lock.

1. From home, tap **Apps** ⊞ > **Settings** ⚙ > **Lock screen and security** 🔒.

❖ The Lock screen and security menu opens.

2. Tap **Screen lock type**.

❖ The Screen lock settings menu opens.

3. Draw your unlock screen pattern, enter your PIN, or enter your password.

4. Tap **None**.

❖ The screen lock is disabled.

Device Security

Configure security for your phone.

1. From home, tap **Apps** ▦ > **Settings** ⚙ > **Lock screen and security** 🔒.

❖ The Lock screen and security menu opens.

2. Tap **ON/OFF** next to **Unknown sources** to enable installation of non-Google Play applications.

Warning: Enabling installation of third-party applications can cause your device and personal data to be more vulnerable to attacks by unknown sources.

3. Tap **Other security settings**.

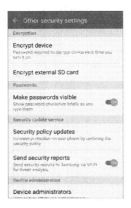

❖ The Other security settings menu opens.

4. Configure the following options:

- **Encrypt device**: Follow the prompts to encrypt all data on your device.

- **Encrypt external SD card**: Follow the prompts to encrypt all data on your optional memory card (not included).

- **Make passwords visible**: Display password characters briefly as you type them.

- **Security policy updates**: Automatically or manually check for security policy updates.

- **Send security reports**: Send security reports to Samsung using Wi-Fi for threat analysis.

- **Device administrators**: Manage your device administrators and application installation privileges.

- **Storage type**: Select a storage location for credential contents.

- **View security certificates**: Display certificates in your device's ROM and other certificates you have installed.

- **Install from device storage**: Install a new certificate from storage.

- **Clear credentials**: Erase the credential contents from the device and reset the password.

- **Trust agents**: Perform selected actions when trusted devices are connected.

- **Pin windows**: Pin an app on your device screen, preventing access to other features of your phone.

- **Usage data access**: View the applications that can access your device's usage history.

- **Notification access**: View the applications that can access notifications you receive on your phone.

Note: To view Trust agents, set up a secure screen lock (Password, PIN, or Pattern). For more information, see Screen Lock.

Privacy

Privacy and safety features include locating methods and diagnostic reporting of your phone. The following settings are available.

Privacy Settings	Description
Location	Select the method used to estimate your location. You can also view the apps that have requested your location and review their history logs.
Report diagnostic info	You can choose to enable reporting of diagnostic info when your phone experiences technical problems.

Access Privacy Settings

- From home, tap **Apps** ⊞ > **Settings** ⚙ > **Privacy** ⊚.

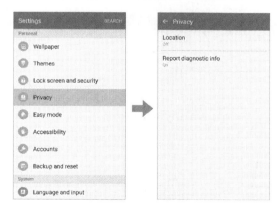

❖ The Privacy and safety menu opens.

Location Settings

Your Location services settings menu lets you select how your phone determines its location (using the wireless networks, GPS satellites, both, or neither).

Enable Location Services

Before using any features that require location assistance, you must enable your phone's Location services.

1. From home, tap **Apps** > **Settings** > **Privacy** .

2. Tap **Location**.

3. Tap **ON/OFF** to enable Location services.

❖ Your phone's Location services are enabled.

▪ If you see a confirmation, follow the prompts to connect.

Changing Location Method

You can change the methods used for determining your location.

Note: Location must be turned on to change locating method.

1. From home, tap **Apps** ⊞ > **Settings** ⚙ > **Privacy** ⬛.

2. Tap **Location**.

3. Tap **Locating method**.

4. Select a locating method. Each mode has a description of which method or methods are used to estimate your location.

   ❖ Your phone's Locating method is set.

Location Services

Google uses Location Reporting to store and use your device's most recent location data. Google apps, such as Google Maps, can use this data to improve your search results based on places that you have visited.

1. From home, tap **Apps** ⊞ > **Settings** ⊙ > **Privacy** 🔘.

2. Tap **Location**.

3. Tap **Google Location History** and sign in to your Google Account for more options.

Report Diagnostic Info

You can choose to enable reporting of diagnostic info when your phone experiences technical problems.

Enable Report Diagnostic Info

1. From home, tap **Apps** ⬛ > **Settings** ⚙ > **Privacy** 🔒.

2. Tap **Report diagnostic info**.

3. Read the consent information and tap **Yes** to enable.

Easy Mode

Easy mode provides a simpler experience using your phone, with a simpler home screen layout and simpler app interactions. If you are a first-time smartphone user, or just to want to simplify the operation of your phone, you can turn on Easy mode at any time.

Easy Mode Overview

The following Easy mode options may be configured:

Easy mode Option	Description
Standard mode	Use the standard home screen layout.
Easy mode	Use a simpler home screen layout and straight forward application interactions. The font size Large will be applied throughout the device.

Enable Easy Mode

1. From home, tap **Apps** ▦ > **Settings** ⚙ > **Easy mode** 🔄.

2. Tap **Easy mode**, and then select the apps you want to use from the Easy applications list.

3. Tap **Done** to apply your Easy mode settings.

Return to Standard Mode

You can use the Easy mode Settings menu to return to Standard mode.

1. From home, swipe the screen to the left and tap **Settings** 🔯 > **Easy mode** ⬤.

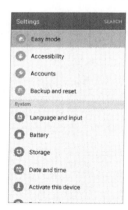

2. Tap **Standard mode** and then tap **Done**.

Accessibility Settings

The Accessibility menu lets you enable and manage accessibility-related applications.

Accessibility Settings Overview

The following Accessibility options may be configured:

Accessibility Option	Description
Vision	Configure accessibility features for vision.
Hearing	Configure accessibility features for hearing and sounds.
Dexterity and interaction	Configure accessibility features for handling and interactions with the phone.
Direct access	Open your accessibility settings by pressing the Home key three times in quick succession.
Notification reminder	Set the phone to beep or vibrate at set intervals to remind you of any unread notifications from selected applications.
Answering and ending calls	Answer calls by pressing the Home key, and end calls by pressing the Power/Lock key.
Single tap mode	Dismiss or snooze alarms, calendar events, and timer alerts, and answer or reject incoming calls with a single tap.

Accessibility Option	Description
TalkBack	Receive spoken feedback describing what you touch, select, or activate.
Switch Access	Control your device using configurable key combinations.

Access Accessibility Options

1. From home, tap **Apps** ⊞ > **Settings** ⚙ > **Accessibility** .

2. Set available accessibility options.

   ❖ Your Accessibility settings are applied and saved.

Vision Accessibility Settings

Your phone offers many features to assist users who are blind or low-vision.

1. From home, tap **Apps** 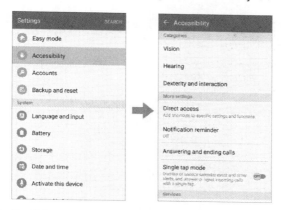 > **Settings** > **Accessibility** .

2. Tap **Vision** to configure options:

- **Dark screen**: Keeps your phone's screen turned off at all times. When Dark screen is enabled, double-press the **Power/Lock** key to turn it on or off while using your phone.

- **Rapid key input**: Release your finger to enter a selection, instead of double-tapping it. By default, when you have TalkBack turned on, you must double-tap items on the screen to select them. If you turn on Rapid key input, you can tap and release your finger to select and item instead of double-tapping.

- **Speak passwords**: The phone reads out characters entered in password fields. Use caution with this feature, because others near you will be able to hear your passwords.

- **Font size**: Choose the size of text for your phone's screens.

- **Magnification gestures**: Control zoom and pan options with specific gestures such as triple-tapping, double pinching, and dragging two fingers across the screen.

- **Grayscale**: Display screens in grayscale instead of color.

- **Negative colors**: Screen colors are reversed.

- **Color adjustment**: Adjusts the color of the screen if you have difficulty reading the screen because of the color. Follow the prompts to fine-tune screen colors.

- **Accessibility shortcut**: Quickly turns on accessibility features by pressing and holding the **Power/Lock** key until you hear a sound or feel a vibration, and then pressing and holding with two fingers until you hear an audio confirmation.

- **Text-to-speech options**: Configure options for converting text to speech.

Hearing Accessibility Settings

Your phone offers many features to assist users who are deaf or hearing-impaired.

1. From home, tap **Apps** ▦ > **Settings** ⚙ > **Accessibility** ◉.

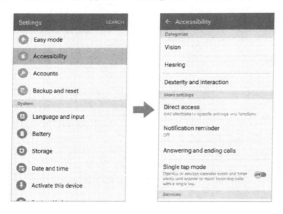

2. Tap **Hearing** to configure options:

- **Flash notification**: Flash the camera light when you receive notifications or when alarms sound. Turn the device over to stop the flashing.

- **Turn off all sounds**: Sounds made by the phone during taps, selections, notifications, are muted.

- **Hearing aids**: Automatically adjusts to attempt to improve the sound quality for use with hearing aids.

- **Samsung subtitles (CC)**: Displays Samsung subtitles where available. Tap **ON/OFF** to turn the option on or off, and then configure options.

- **Google subtitles (CC)**: Displays Google subtitles where available. Tap **ON/OFF** to turn the option on or off, and then configure options like Language, Text size, and Caption style.

- **Left/right sound balance**: Adjust the sound sent to the left and right when using earphones.

- **Mono audio**: Enable or disable the compression of stereo audio into a single mono audio stream for use with a single earphone.

Dexterity and Interaction Settings

Your phone offers many features to improve accessibility related to the way you interact with touch and movement.

1. From home, tap **Apps** 🎬 > **Settings** ⚙️ > **Accessibility** ♿.

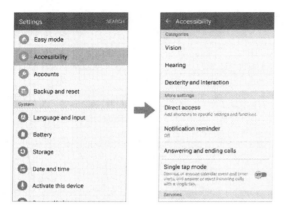

2. Tap **Dexterity and interaction** to configure this option:

- **Assistant menu**: Assistant menu can improve phone accessibility by providing quick access to important functions. A shortcut ▦ appears on all screens to give you access to the Assistant menu. Tap **Assistant menu** to configure options:

    - Tap **ON/OFF** beside Assistant menu to turn the feature on or off. When you turn on Assistant menu, Single tap mode is also enabled.

    - **Dominant hand**: Choose whether the Assistant menu displays on the left or right side of the screen

    - **Edit**: Re-order or remove items from the Assistant menu.

- **Assistant plus**: When turned on, Assistant plus displays contextual menu options for some apps in Assistant menu. Not all apps support this option. Tap **Assistant plus**, and then tap **ON/OFF** to turn the option on or off. After you turn on Assistant plus, enable or disable apps to use with Assistant plus.

- **Touchpad size**: Choose a size for touchpads for use in your phone's screens.

- **Cursor size**: Choose the size of cursors, to display on the screen.

- **Cursor speed**: Choose a speed for cursor blinks.

- **Press and hold delay**: Choose how long your phone waits during a touch and hold gesture on the screen before continuing with the touch and hold action.

- **Interaction control**: Control how your phone interprets motions and screen touches. To turn Interaction control on or off at any time, press and hold the **Home** key and the down **Volume** key at the same time. When Interaction control is on, you can use motions to control your phone, and screen timeout is turned on. You can also block areas of the screen from touch interaction. Automatic screen rotation and hard-key functions (**Power/Lock** key, **Volume** key, and more) will be turned off, and app notifications will only be shown in the notification panel and status bar.

Configure Other Accessibility Settings

Your phone offers many features to improve phone accessibility.

1. From home, tap **Apps** ⊞ > **Settings** ⚙ > **Accessibility** ◑.

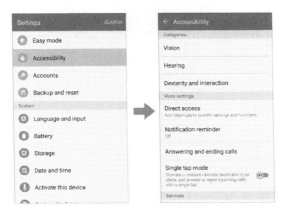

2. Configure additional accessibility options:

    - **Direct access**: Access common accessibility settings from any screen by pressing the **Home** key rapidly 3 times in a row.

- **Notification reminder**: Set the phone to alert you using vibration or sound to remind you of unread notifications.

- **Answering and ending calls**: Select options for answering and ending calls.

  - **Pressing the Home key**: Answer calls by pressing the **Home** key.

  - **Pressing the Power key**: End calls by pressing the **Power/Lock** key.

- **Single tap mode**: Use a single tap to dismiss or snooze alarms, notifications and alerts, and answer or reject calls.

- **TalkBack**: Receive spoken feedback describing what you touch, select, or activate.

- **Switch Access**: Control your device using configurable key combinations.

Note: Additional accessibility services you have installed are displayed under the **Services** heading.

Add Accounts

The Accounts settings menu lets you add and manage all your email, social networking, and picture and video sharing accounts.

Set Up a New Account

1. From home, tap **Apps** ⚏ > **Settings** ⚙ > **Accounts** .

2. Tap **Add account**.

❖ An Add account window appears.

3. Tap an account type and then follow the prompts to add the required account information.

❖ The account is added to the accounts list.

Manage Existing Accounts

1. From home, tap **Apps** ▦ > **Settings** ⚙ > **Accounts** ⊙.

2. Tap the account type to see the existing accounts.

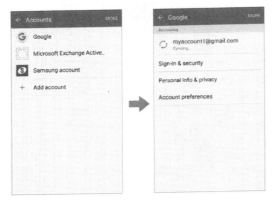

❖ The Account settings menu appears.

3. View and configure your account settings as desired.

❖ The Account options are updated.

Backup and Reset

Your phone's Backup and reset menu lets you back up your phone's data and settings to Google servers before resetting your phone to the original factory settings. The Factory data reset erases all data from the phone's application storage, including:

- Your Samsung account

- Your Google Account

- All other email and social networking accounts

- System and application data and settings

- Downloaded applications

Backup and Reset Overview

The following options are available in the Back up and reset menu:

Backup and Reset Option	Description
Backup account	Select the Google Account used to back up data.

Backup and Reset Option	Description
Back up my data	Enable backup for application data, Wi-Fi passwords, and other settings to your Google Account.
Automatic restore	When reinstalling an application, backed up settings and data will be restored from your Google Account.
Reset settings	Reset all settings to their factory defaults except the security, language, and account settings. Your personal data and the settings of downloaded apps will not be affected.
Factory data reset	Reset all settings and delete all data on phone.

- Performing a Factory data reset erases all data on the phone. It is recommended that you back up important data before performing a factory data reset.

- Erased information cannot be restored. Only erase data after you are sure you have saved everything you need.

Access Backup and Reset Options

1. From home, tap **Apps** ▦ > **Settings** ⚙ > **Backup and reset** ⦿.

❖ The Backup and reset menu opens.

2. Set options.

❖ The Backup and reset settings are applied and saved.

▪ If you are performing a Factory data reset, follow the prompts to confirm the data removal. The phone will erase all data and reboot.

Factory Data Reset

Return your device to its factory defaults.

Factory Reset Protection

Adding a Google Account to your device automatically enables the Factory Reset Protection (FRP) security feature.

FRP prevents other people from using your device if it is reset to factory settings without your permission. For example, if your device is lost or stolen, only someone with your Google Account can perform a factory data reset and use the device.

When a device is factory reset, the device will not be able to be setup without the user entering the Google Account associated with the device.

Caution: You should remove your Google Account before shipping your device to Samsung or any other service provider for service and before resetting the device to factory settings.

Important: Before initiating a Factory Reset on your own, confirm your Google Username and password are up to date and active. You will need this information upon restart of the device.

To reset your device to its factory defaults:

1. From home, tap **Apps** ⊞ > **Settings** ⚙ > **Backup and reset** 🖺.

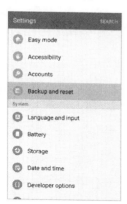

❖ The Backup and reset menu opens.

2. Tap **Factory data reset**.

3. Read the factory data reset information page and tap **Reset device**.

4. If prompted, enter your current pattern, PIN, or password.

5. Tap **Delete all**.

❖ Your phone will power down and reset itself.

▪ Once the phone has reset, it will run through the Hands Free Activation and update processes again. When finished, you will see the Welcome screen and Setup application. See Complete the Setup Screens to start over.

Warning: This action permanently erases ALL data from the device, including Google or other account settings, system and application data and settings, downloaded applications, as well as your music, photos, videos, and other files.

Language and Input Settings

Your phone's Language and input settings let you select a language for the phone's menus and keyboards, select and configure keyboard settings, configure speech input settings, and set your phone's mouse/trackpad options.

Language and Input Settings Overview

You can set the following options in the Language and input settings menu:

Language and Input Setting	Description
Language	Set the language for your display and menus.
Default keyboard	Set the default method for entering text.
Samsung keyboard	Set Samsung keyboard options.
Google voice typing	Set options for Google Voice text entry.
Voice input	Set your voice search options.
Text-to-speech options	Set Text-to-speech options.
Pointer speed	Set the speed of the pointer for a mouse/trackpad.

Access Language and Input Setting Options

1. From home, tap **Apps** ▦ > **Settings** ⚙ > **Language and input** ⒶⒶ.

❖ The Language and input settings menu opens.

2. Set options.

❖ The Language and input settings are applied and saved.

Select the Default Language for Your Phone

1. From home, tap **Apps** ▦ > **Settings** ⚙ > **Language and input** Ⓐ.

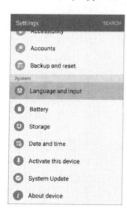

2. Tap **Language**.

3. Tap an available language.

Language and Input Options

Some of the Language and input options are detailed below.

1. From home, tap **Apps** > **Settings** > **Language and input**.

2. Set options:

- **Language**: Tap a language to assign it.

- **Default keyboard**: Tap an input method to set it as the default.

- **Samsung keyboard**: Configure your keyboard options.

- **Google voice typing**: Configure your options, including language detection.

- **Voice input**: Tap a settings option and follow the prompts.

- **Text-to-speech**: Tap a settings option and follow the prompts.

- **Pointer speed**: Drag the bar to adjust the speed, and then tap **OK**.

Battery Settings

Monitor your phone's battery usage through this settings menu. View which functions are consuming your battery's charge and at what percentage. You can also display the battery charge remaining as a percentage on the status bar.

1. From home, tap **Apps**  > **Settings** ⚙ > **Battery** 🔋.

2. Tap **Display battery percentage** to show the percentage of battery charge remaining on the status bar.

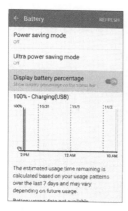

3. Tap items to view details.

   ❖ Check your battery condition and access additional options.

Power Saving Mode

Save battery power by activating Power saving mode, which reduces or turns off certain features to decrease battery consumption.

Turn On Power Saving Mode

1. From home, tap **Apps** ⊞ > **Settings** ⚙ > **Battery** ⭘.

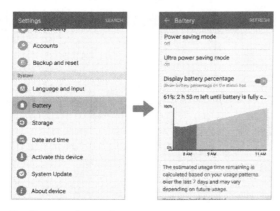

2. Tap **Power saving mode**.

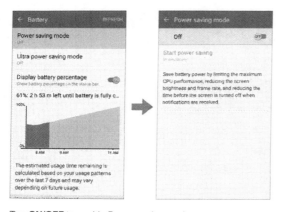

3. Tap **ON/OFF** to enable Power saving mode.

   ❖ Power saving mode is activated.

4. Tap **Start power saving** to enable Power saving mode immediately, or at a selected percentage of battery power.

Ultra Power Saving Mode

Conserve power and extend your phone's battery life by using a minimal home screen layout, limiting the number of usable apps, turning off mobile data when the screen is off, and turning off connectivity features such as Wi-Fi and Bluetooth.

Turn On Ultra Power Saving Mode

1. From home, tap **Apps** ⊞ > **Settings** ⚙ > **Battery** ◯.

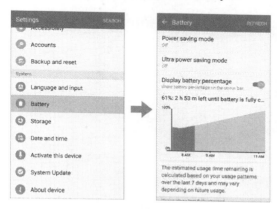

2. Tap **Ultra power saving mode**.

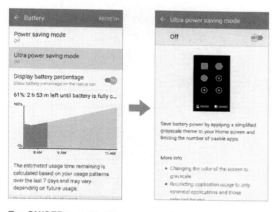

3. Tap **ON/OFF** to enable Ultra power saving mode.

   ❖ Ultra power saving mode is activated.

Turn Off Ultra Power Saving Mode

■ From home, tap **More** > **Turn off Ultra power saving mode**.

❖ The phone returns to normal power mode.

Storage Settings

The Storage settings menu lets you manage internal storage on your phone.

Storage Settings Overview

The sound settings menu allows you to configure the following options:

Storage Device	Description
Device memory	• **Total space**: View the total space/free space in your phone's memory.
	• **Available space**: The amount of storage space currently available.
	• **System memory**: The minimum amount of storage space required to run the system.
	• **Used space**: The amount of storage space currently being used.
	• **Cached data**: The amount of data currently cached.
	• **Miscellaneous files**: The amount of memory used to store miscellaneous files.

Access Storage Settings

1. From home, tap **Apps** 🎛 > **Settings** ⚙ > **Storage** ⊕.

2. View memory usage for the different types of information stored in your phone's memory. Tap an item for more information.

microSD Card

A microSD memory card is an optional accessory (not included) that allows you to store images, videos, music, documents, and other data on your phone.

Important: You can damage a microSD card by improper installation. Please be careful when inserting, removing, or handling it.

Install a microSD Card

Follow the instructions below to install an optional memory card (not included).

1. Remove the back cover.

    - Grasp the phone firmly and locate the slot at the top of the phone.

    - Place your fingernail in the opening and firmly "pop" the cover off the phone.

2. With the gold contacts facing down, slide the card into the slot.

3. Replace the back cover.

Remove a microSD Card

Use the following procedures to remove an optional microSD card from your phone.

1. Remove the back cover.

    - Grasp the phone firmly and locate the slot at the top of the phone.

    - Place your fingernail in the opening and firmly "pop" the cover off the phone.

2. Remove the card from the slot.

3. Replace the back cover.

View microSD Card Memory

Use the following procedure to view memory usage information for an optional installed microSD card (not included).

- From home, tap **Apps** ⊞ > **Settings** ⚙ > **Storage**.

    ❖ The total and available memory space will be displayed.

Format a microSD Card

Formatting a microSD card permanently removes all files stored on the card.

1. From home, tap **Apps** 🏭 > **Settings** 🖳 > **Storage**.

2. Scroll down the screen, tap **Format SD card** > **Format SD card** > **Delete all**.

Note: Formatting erases all the data on an installed microSD card, after which the files CANNOT be retrieved. To prevent the loss of important data, please check the contents before you format the card.

Unmount a microSD Card

When you need to remove an optional installed microSD card, you must unmount the card first to prevent corrupting the data stored on it or damaging the card.

1. From home, tap **Apps** 🏭 > **Settings** 🖳 > **Storage**.

2. Tap **Unmount SD card**.

3. Remove the microSD card. See Remove a microSD Card.

Date and Time Settings

Use the Date and Time settings menu either to automatically use the network-provided date and time or manually set these values, as well as select time and date format options.

Date and Time Overview

The following Date and time options may be configured:

Date and Time Option	Description
Automatic date and time	Set the date and time automatically using the connected wireless network.
Automatic time zone	Set the time zone automatically using the connected wireless network.
Set date	Set the date manually (only available when Automatic date and time option is disabled).
Set time	Set the time manually (only available when Automatic date and time option is disabled).
Select time zone	Set the time zone manually (only when Automatic time zone is disabled).
Use 24-hour format	Enable or disable 24-hour time format.

Access Date and Time Options

1. From home, tap **Apps** ▦ > **Settings** ⚙ > **Date and time** 🕐.

2. Set available date and time options.

 ❖ Your date and time settings are applied and saved.

Activate This Device

The Activate this device menu lets you activate a new phone or use additional self-service options such as checking the status of an in-service phone.

1. From home, tap **Apps** 🏾 > **Settings** ⚙ > **Activate this device** 🔘.

 ❖ The Self Service menu appears.

2. Follow the prompts to activate your phone or review your summary.

 ❖ Your phone activates. If already activated on an account, you will see a usage and plan summary.

System Update

The System Update menu provides settings for keeping your phone up-to-date with the latest software.

Access System Update

■ From home, tap **Apps** 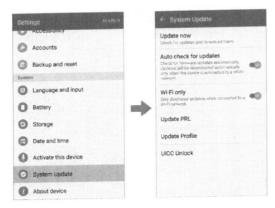 > **Settings** > **System Update** .

❖ The System Update menu appears.

For details about updating your phone, see Update Your Phone.

About Device

The About device menu lets you access important phone information, search for and apply updates, and view legal and safety information.

About Device Overview

The following About device items may be reviewed or set:

About Device Item	Description
Software version	Check your current software version.
Hardware version	Check your current hardware version.

About Device Item	Description
Status	Check your phone's status. • Battery status and level • SIM card status (network, signal strength, mobile network type, service state, roaming, mobile network state, phone number, IMEI number, and IMEISV number) • IMEI information (MIN, PRL version, MEID, IMEI, and ICCID) • IP address • Wi-Fi MAC address • Bluetooth address • Up time • Device status
Legal information	Review various types of important legal information, including Open source licenses, Google legal information, System WebView licenses, Wallpapers, Samsung legal information, and the Privacy Alert.
Device name	Change the name of your device (other devices see this name when using Mobile Hotspot or Bluetooth).
Model number	Check the phone's model number.
Android version	Check the Android version number.
Android security patch level	Check the Android security patch version.
Baseband version	Check the phone's baseband version.
Kernel version	Check the phone's kernel version.
Build number	Check the current phone build number.
SE for Android status	Check the phone's SE for Android status.
KNOX version	Check the current KNOX version.

Access About Device Options

1. From home, tap **Apps**  > **Settings** > **About device** .

2. Select or view available options.

❖ Your phone information is displayed.

For Assistance

The following topics address areas of support for your phone, including troubleshooting, specifications, account information, warranty information, and customer service contact information.

Boost Account Information and Help

Find out about managing your account online and on your phone, buying additional minutes for your plan, and getting help.

For more information about your Boost Mobile account, as well as other Boost Mobile services, visit us at: boostmobile.com.

Manage Your Account

Access information about your account. You can:

- Check your minutes.
- Re-Boost® (add money to your account).
- Change plans.
- And more.

From Your Phone

Access account information and other self-service tools from Boost Zone.

- From home, tap **Apps** ▦ > **Boost Zone** ▦.

You can also dial directly for access to certain information:

- Dial # 2 2 5 (**#BAL**) to check account balance.
- Dial # 2 3 3 (**#ADD**) to make a payment.
- Dial # 6 1 1 to launch Boost Zone or call Boost Customer Care (depending on your Settings) to get answers to other questions.

From Your Computer

- Visit boostmobile.com, click **My Account**, and log in with your wireless phone number and account PIN.

From Any Other Phone

- Boost Customer Care: **1-888-BOOST-4U** (1-888-266-7848).

Re-Boost

Boost Mobile makes it easy to add money to your account. You decide exactly how and where you want to pay. Keep your account active by using your phone and adding money to your account.

Pay with Cash

Find an Authorized Re-Boost Retailer near you. Pick up a Re-Boost Card or recharge for as low as $10 at the register, where available.

Pay Anytime with a Credit/Debit Card

Dial # 2 3 3 (#ADD) to add money from your phone, or visit **My Account** at boostmobile.com to do it online. Securely register your credit/debit card with Boost for more convenient one-time payments or to set up easy Auto Re-Boost payments.

Set Up Worry-Free Payments with Auto Re-Boost^{SM}

It is the easiest way to make sure your account stays on and active. Use a credit card, debit card or bank account—whatever is best for you.

Visit boostmobile.com/reboost to get the details on all your Re-Boost options.

Samsung KNOX

Samsung KNOX™ is Samsung's security platform and is a mark for a Samsung device tested for security with enterprise use in mind. Additional licensing fee may be required. For more information about Knox, please refer to: samsung.com/us/knox [030115]

Legal Information

Important legal information can be accessed in writing on the mobile device or at samsung.com

READ THIS INFORMATION BEFORE USING YOUR MOBILE DEVICE.

Samsung Limited Warranty - This product is covered under the applicable Samsung Limited Warranty **including its dispute resolution procedure**.

Full written terms and detailed information about the warranty and obtaining service are available on the device at: **Settings > About device > Legal Information > Samsung legal** or you may access the online version of the Health/Safety and Warranty guide for your device at:

English
samsung.com/us/Legal/Phone-HSGuide

Spanish
samsung.com/us/Legal/Phone-HSGuide-SP

The online version of the End User License Agreement (EULA) for your device can be found online at: samsung.com/us/Legal/SamsungLegal-EULA4

For Assistance

WARNING: This product contains chemicals known to the State of California to cause cancer, birth defects, or other reproductive harm. For more information, please call 1-800-SAMSUNG (726-7864).

Note: Screen images are simulated. Appearance of device may vary.

Samsung Electronics America (SEA), Inc.

Address:
85 Challenger Road
Ridgefield Park,
New Jersey 07660

Phone:
1-800-SAMSUNG (726-7864)

Internet Address:
samsung.com

Disclaimer of Warranties; Exclusion of Liability

EXCEPT AS SET FORTH IN THE EXPRESS WARRANTY CONTAINED ON THE WARRANTY PAGE ENCLOSED WITH THE PRODUCT, THE PURCHASER TAKES THE PRODUCT "AS IS", AND SAMSUNG MAKES NO EXPRESS OR IMPLIED WARRANTY OF ANY KIND WHATSOEVER WITH RESPECT TO THE PRODUCT, INCLUDING BUT NOT LIMITED TO THE MERCHANTABILITY OF THE PRODUCT OR ITS FITNESS FOR ANY PARTICULAR PURPOSE OR USE; THE DESIGN, CONDITION OR QUALITY OF THE PRODUCT; THE PERFORMANCE OF THE PRODUCT; THE WORKMANSHIP OF THE PRODUCT OR THE COMPONENTS CONTAINED THEREIN; OR COMPLIANCE OF THE PRODUCT WITH THE REQUIREMENTS OF ANY LAW, RULE, SPECIFICATION OR CONTRACT PERTAINING THERETO. NOTHING CONTAINED IN THE INSTRUCTION MANUAL SHALL BE CONSTRUED TO CREATE AN EXPRESS OR IMPLIED WARRANTY OF ANY KIND WHATSOEVER WITH RESPECT TO THE PRODUCT. IN ADDITION, SAMSUNG SHALL NOT BE LIABLE FOR ANY DAMAGES OF ANY KIND RESULTING FROM THE PURCHASE OR USE OF THE PRODUCT OR ARISING FROM THE BREACH OF THE EXPRESS WARRANTY, INCLUDING INCIDENTAL, SPECIAL OR CONSEQUENTIAL DAMAGES, OR LOSS OF ANTICIPATED PROFITS OR BENEFITS.

Modification of Software

SAMSUNG IS NOT LIABLE FOR PERFORMANCE ISSUES OR INCOMPATIBILITIES CAUSED BY YOUR EDITING OF REGISTRY SETTINGS, OR YOUR MODIFICATION OF OPERATING SYSTEM SOFTWARE. USING CUSTOM OPERATING SYSTEM SOFTWARE MAY CAUSE YOUR DEVICE AND APPLICATIONS TO WORK IMPROPERLY. YOUR CARRIER MAY NOT PERMIT USERS TO DOWNLOAD CERTAIN SOFTWARE, SUCH AS CUSTOM OS.

Intellectual Property

All Intellectual Property, as defined below, owned by or which is otherwise the property of Samsung or its respective suppliers relating to the SAMSUNG Phone, including but not limited to, accessories, parts, or software relating thereto (the "Phone System"), is proprietary to Samsung and protected under federal laws, state laws, and international treaty provisions. Intellectual Property includes, but is not limited to, inventions (patentable or unpatentable), patents, trade secrets, copyrights, software, computer programs, and related documentation and other works of authorship. You may not infringe or otherwise violate the

For Assistance

330

rights secured by the Intellectual Property. Moreover, you agree that you will not (and will not attempt to) modify, prepare derivative works of, reverse engineer, decompile, disassemble, or otherwise attempt to create source code from the software. No title to or ownership in the Intellectual Property is transferred to you. All applicable rights of the Intellectual Property shall remain with SAMSUNG and its suppliers.

Open Source Software

Some software components of this product incorporate source code covered under GNU General Public License (GPL), GNU Lesser General Public License (LGPL), OpenSSL License, BSD License and other open source licenses. To obtain the source code covered under the open source licenses, please visit: opensource.samsung.com

Copyright Information

Do you have questions about your Samsung Mobile Device?

For 24 hour information and assistance, we offer a new FAQ/ARS System (Automated Response System) at: samsung.com/us/support

The actual available capacity of the internal memory is less than the specified capacity because the operating system and default applications occupy part of the memory. The available capacity may change when you upgrade the device.

Nuance®, VSuite™, T9® Text Input, and the Nuance logo are trademarks or registered trademarks of Nuance Communications, Inc., or its affiliates in the United States and/or other countries.

The Bluetooth® word mark, figure mark (stylized "B Design"), and combination mark (Bluetooth word mark and "B Design") are registered trademarks and are wholly owned by the Bluetooth SIG.

microSD™ and the microSD logo are Trademarks of the SD Card Association.

Google, the Google logo, Android, the Android logo, Google Play, Gmail, Google Mail, Google Maps, Google Music, Google Now, Chrome, Google Hangouts, Picasa, YouTube, and other marks are trademarks of Google Inc.

Wi-Fi is a registered trademark of the Wireless Fidelity Alliance, Inc.

Index